for GCSE

Book F2 part A

PUBLISHED BY THE PRESS SYNDICATE OF THE UNIVERSITY OF CAMBRIDGE
The Pitt Building, Trumpington Street, Cambridge, United Kingdom

CAMBRIDGE UNIVERSITY PRESS
The Edinburgh Building, Cambridge CB2 2RU, UK
40 West 20th Street, New York, NY 10011-4211, USA
477 Williamstown Road, Port Melbourne, VIC 3207, Australia
Ruiz de Alarcón 13, 28014 Madrid, Spain
Dock House, The Waterfront, Cape Town 8001, South Africa

http://www.cambridge.org

© The School Mathematics Project 2002
First published 2002

Printed in Italy by Rotolito Lombarda
Typeface Minion   *System* QuarkXPress®

A catalogue record for this book is available from the British Library.

ISBN 0 521 01283 X   paperback

Typesetting and technical illustrations by The School Mathematics Project
Illustration on page 17 by Dave Parker

Acknowledgements

The authors and publishers are grateful to the following Examination Boards for permission to reproduce questions from past examination papers:

AQA(NEAB)	Assessment and Qualifications Alliance
AQA(SEG)	Assessment and Qualifications Alliance
Edexcel	Edexcel Foundation
OCR	Oxford, Cambridge and RSA Examinations
WJEC	Welsh Joint Education Committee

Data on page 92 from National Statistics. Crown copyright material is reproduced with the permission of the Controller of HMSO and the Queen's Printer for Scotland.

NOTICE TO TEACHERS
It is illegal to reproduce any part of this work in material form (including photocopying and electronic storage) except under the following circumstances:
(i) where you are abiding by a licence granted to your school or institution by the Copyright Licensing Agency;
(ii) where no such licence exists, or where you wish to exceed the terms of a licence, and you have gained the written permission of Cambridge University Press;
(iii) where you are allowed to reproduce without permission under the provisions of Chapter 3 of the Copyright, Designs and Patents Act 1988.

Contents

1	Graphs from rules	4
2	Calculating with decimals 1	13
3	2D puzzles	21
4	Areas of triangles	31
5	Trial and improvement	39
6	3D puzzles	46
7	Solving equations	56
8	Finding and using formulas	64
	Review 1	72
9	Ratio and proportion	74
10	Metric measures	87
11	Looking at data 1	92
12	Negative numbers	104
13	Percentage calculations 1	112
14	Coordinates	120
15	Using a calculator 1	126
16	Brackets	132
17	Pie charts	139
	Review 2	151

1 Graphs from rules

You will revise
- plotting points using a formula
- reading scales on graphs

The work will help you to learn
- how to plot points and draw the graph of a straight line, given its equation
- how to read off the coordinates of points on a straight line

A Revising the plot

A1 When p is 10, we can work out the value of $2p - 3$ like this:
Work out the value of each of these expressions when $p = 10$.

(a) $3p + 1$ (b) $5 + 2p$ (c) $5p - 20$
(d) $45 - p$ (e) $50 - 2p$ (f) $5 + 4p$

> $2p - 3$ when $p = 10$
> $= 2 \times 10 - 3$
> $= 20 - 3$
> $= 17$

A2 This graph converts between the volume of ice-cream in litres and its weight in kilograms.

(a) How much does 1 litre of ice-cream weigh?
(b) What is the weight of 1.5 litres of ice-cream?
(c) What is the **volume** of 2 kg of ice-cream?

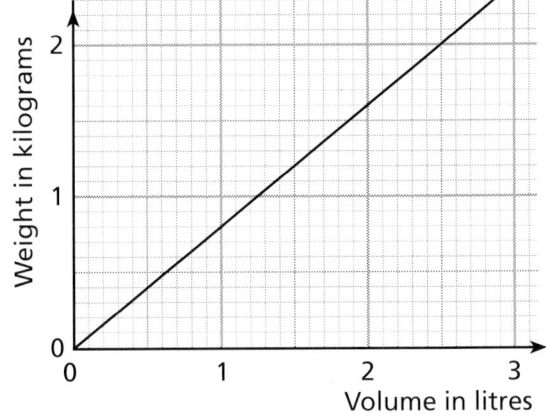

A3 This graph shows how the weight of copper tubing varies with its length.

(a) How many kilograms will a 2 metre piece of tubing weigh?
(b) What will a 3 m tube weigh?
(c) One piece of tubing weighs 9.5 kg. How long is it?
(d) How much will a piece of tubing weigh that is 1 m 50 cm long?
(e) How much will a 6 m tube weigh?

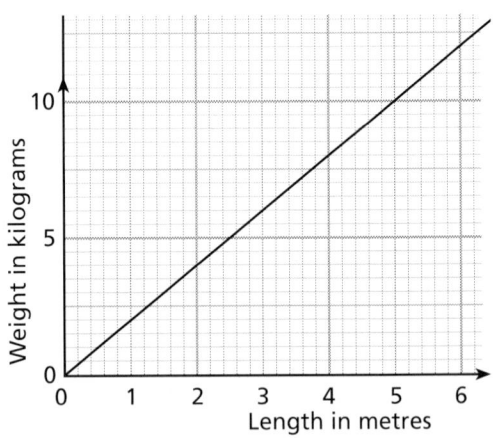

A4 A rough rule for working out a person's height is

height in centimetres = 3 × distance round head in centimetres

(a) Copy and complete this table using the rule.

Distance round head in cm	40	45	50	55	60	65
Height in cm	120	135				

(b) Draw axes like the ones on the right.

Plot the points from your table.
Join them with a line.

Use your graph to answer these.

(c) The distance round Harry's head is 58 cm.
How tall does the graph say he is?

(d) Aifa's height is 140 centimetres.
What is the distance round her head?

(e) Chloë is 165 cm tall.
Would a bandage 120 cm long go round her head twice?

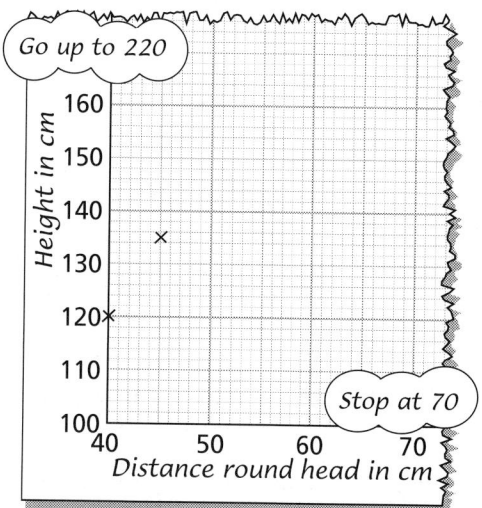

A5 When a lorry dumps waste at a tip, it has to pay.
A computer works out the charge.

At Waterdale tip, the formula the computer uses is $c = 35 + 10w$
c is the charge in £; w is the weight of rubbish tipped in tonnes.

(a) A lorry tips 4 tonnes.
Copy and complete this to work out the charge. $c = 35 + 10 \times 4 = ...$

(b) A lorry tips 12 tonnes. How much will it cost?

(c) Copy and complete this table.

Weight of rubbish (w)	2	4	6	8	10	12
Charge in pounds (c)	55					

(d) Draw and label axes like the ones on the right.

Plot the points from your table.
Join them with a line.

Use your graph to answer these.

(e) How much will it cost to tip 7 tonnes of rubbish?

(f) How much will it cost to tip 5 tonnes?

(g) Bob paid £130 to tip rubbish.
How much did his rubbish weigh?

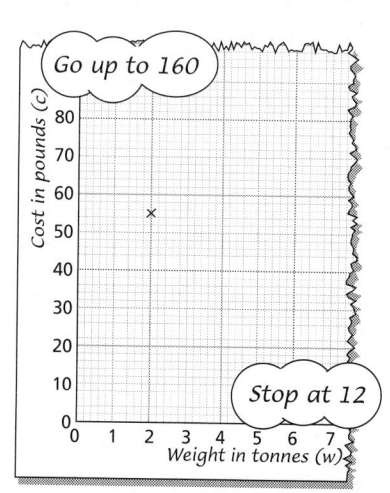

A6 A spring stretches when objects are hung from it. The formula for its length is

$l = 2w + 16$

w is the weight in kg.
l is the length of the spring in cm.

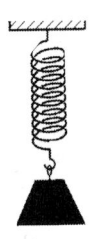

OCR(MEG)

(a) Copy and complete this table.

w	0	2	4	6	8	10
l	16			28		36

(b) Draw the graph on a copy of the grid on the right.

(c) Jane hangs an object on the spring. She measures the length of the spring. It is 29 cm.

Use your graph to find the weight of the object.

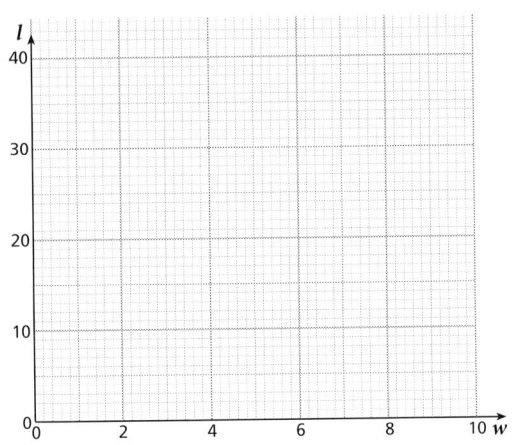

B Finding patterns

x-coordinate (x)	0	1	2	3	4	5
y-coordinate (y)	0	2	4	6	8	10

$y = x + 2$? $y = 2x$

$y = 2$ $x = 2y$

B1 Look at the numbers in this table. Which of the rules below is true?

x-coordinate (x)	0	1	2	3	4	5
y-coordinate (y)	0	3	6	9	12	15

$y = 3$ $x = 3y$ $y = x$ $y = 3x$

B2 Which of the rules below are true for this table?
(More than one is true.)

x-coordinate (x)	0	1	2	3	4	5
y-coordinate (y)	2	3	4	5	6	7

$y = 2$ $x = y - 2$ $y = 2x$ $y = x + 2$

B3 Which of the rules below is true for this table?
Remember it must work for all the pairs of numbers in the table.

x-coordinate (x)	0	1	2	3	4	5
y-coordinate (y)	1	3	5	7	9	11

$y = 3x$ $y = 2x$ $y = 2x + 1$ $y = x + 1$

B4 Here are four rules and four tables. Which rule goes with which table?

$y = 4x$ $y = 2x + 4$ $y = 4x + 1$ $y = 2x + 3$

A

x	0	1	2	3	4	5
y	3	5	7	9	11	13

B

x	0	1	2	3	4	5
y	4	6	8	10	12	14

C

x	0	1	2	3	4	5
y	0	4	8	12	16	20

D

x	0	1	2	3	4	5
y	1	5	9	13	17	21

C Drawing the line

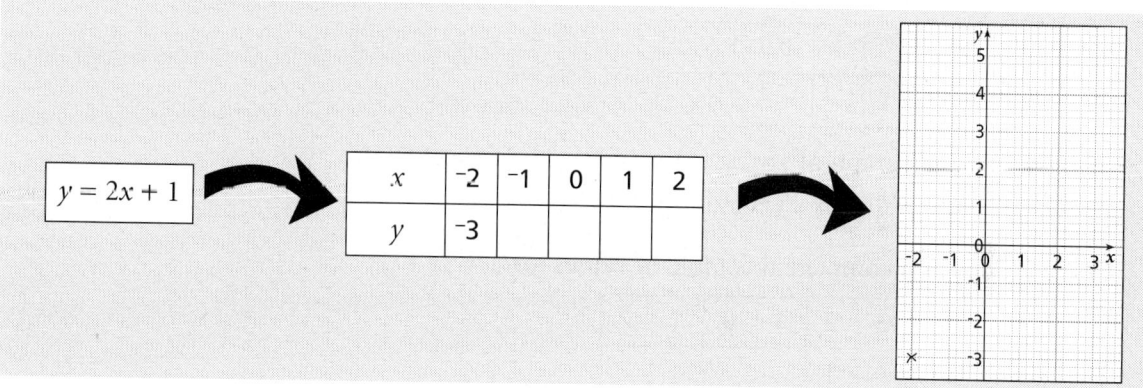

C1 For the rule $y = x + 3$

(a) What is y when $x = 1$?

(b) What is y when $x = 3$?

(c) Copy and complete this table.

x	0	1	2	3	4	5
y	3					

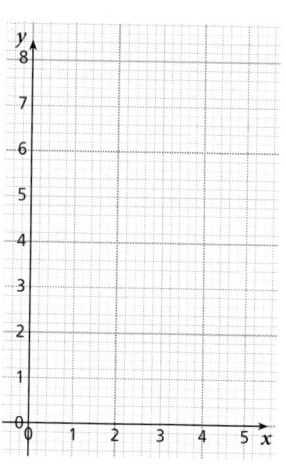

(d) On axes like the ones on the right, plot the points from your table. Join the points with a line.

(e) From the graph, what is y when x is 2.5?

(f) What is the value of x when y is 7.5?

C2 For the rule $y = 2x$

(a) What is y when x is 1?

(b) What is y when x is $^-1$?

(c) Copy and complete this table.

x	-2	-1	0	1	2	3
y	-4					

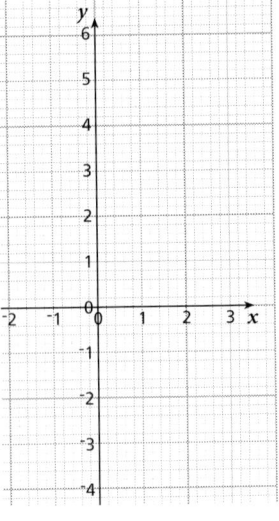

(d) On axes like the ones on the right, plot the points from your table. Join the points with a line.

(e) Copy and complete these coordinates of points on the line.
(0.5, ...)   (2.5, ...)   (......., $^-$3)

C3 This question is on sheet P109.

C4 This question is on sheet P109.

C5 (a) Copy and complete the table for $y = 3x - 1$.

x	-1	0	1	2
$y = 3x - 1$			2	

(b) Draw the graph of $y = 3x - 1$ on the grid on sheet P110.

(c) Find the value of x when $y = 3$.

AQA(SEG) 1999

C6 (a) Copy and complete this table of values for $y = 2x + 3$.

x	-3	-2	-1	0	1	2
y		-1				

(b) Draw the graph of $y = 2x + 3$ on the grid on sheet P110.

(c) Use your graph to find

(i) the value of y when $x = 1.5$

(ii) the value of x when $y = ^-0.5$

Edexcel

C7 Draw the graph of $y = 3x - 2$ on graph paper.
Use values of x from 0 to 5.

OCR

C8 Draw the graph of $y = 2x - 15$ on the grid on sheet P110.

Edexcel

D A different type of equation

- Copy and complete this list of the coordinates of the points marked on the line.

    A (1, ...)
    B (3, ...)
    C (..., ...)
    D (-2, ...)
    E (0, ...)

- What do you notice about the y-coordinates of all the points on the line?
- Which of these equations could be the equation of the line?

    $y = 3$ $x = 3$ $y = x + 3$

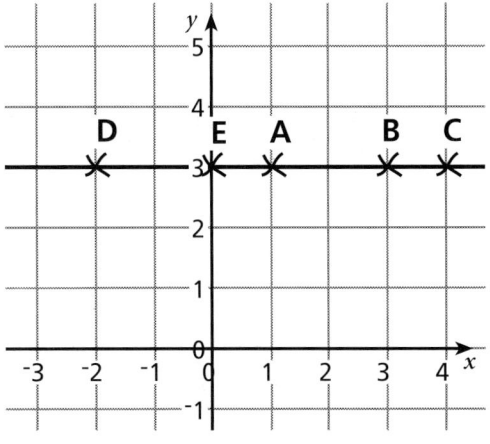

D1 (a) Copy and complete this table for points on the line on this graph.

x	2	2			2
y	-1	0	1	2	3

(b) What do you notice about the coordinates of the points on this line?

(c) Which of these equations could be the equation of this line?

$y = x + 2$ $y = 2$ $x = 2$

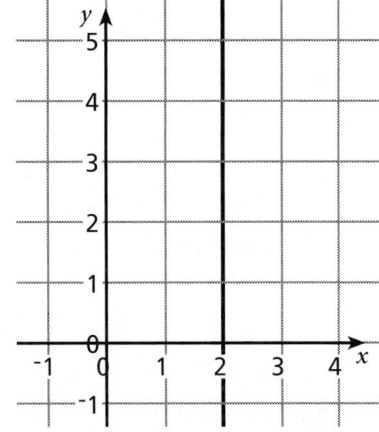

D2 Copy this diagram onto squared paper.

(a) Label each of the lines with its equation. (One line is labelled for you.)

(b) On the same diagram, draw and label the line $y = x$.

(c) What are the coordinates of the point where the line $y = x$ crosses the line $y = -2$?

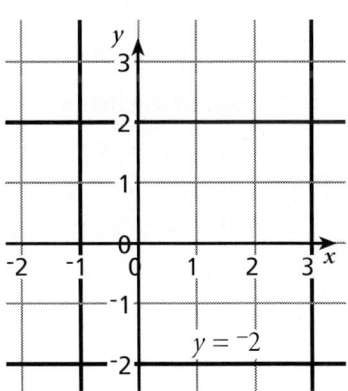

D3 On squared paper, draw x- and y-axes both going from -5 to 5. On your axes, draw and label lines with these equations:

$y = 4$ $x = -3$ $y = -1$ $x = 5$ $y = -4$

E On different lines

To draw the graph of $x + 2y = 12$ we need to find points that fit the equation.
- Can you spot any values of x and y that fit?
- When y is 3, what value of x fits the equation?
  (You need to find x so that $x + 2 \times 3 = 12$.)
- When x is 4, what value of y fits the equation?
- Check that when $y = 0$, $x = 12$.
- When $x = 0$, what value of y fits the equation?
- Copy and complete this table.
- On graph paper draw axes with both x and y going from 0 to 12.

x	0	2	4	6	8	10	12
y							0

- Plot your points and draw the line $x + 2y = 12$

E1 We want to draw the graph of $x + 3y = 6$.
(a) When $y = 0$, then $x + 3 \times 0 = 6$.
What is the value of x?
(b) When $y = 1$ what is x?
(c) Copy and complete this table for $x + 3y = 6$.
(d) On graph paper, draw axes with both x and y going from 0 to 6.

x			
y	0	1	2

Plot the points from the table and draw the line $x + 3y = 6$.
(e) From the graph, what is y when $x = 1.5$?
(f) What is x when $y = 0.5$?

E2 For the formula $x + y = 7$
(a) Copy the table on the right.
(b) (i) Check that when $x = 0$, y is 7.
   (ii) Check that when $y = 0$, x is 7.

x	0	1	2	3	4	5	6	7
y	7							0

(c) When $y = 1$, we get $x + 1 = 7$.
What is the value of x? Make an entry in the table.
(d) When $y = 2$ what is x?
(e) Complete the table.
(f) On graph paper, draw axes with both x and y going from 0 to 8.
Plot the points from the table.
Draw and label the line $x + y = 7$.
(g) Copy and complete these coordinates for points on the line.

(2.5, ...)   (....., 5.5)

E3 Follow these steps to draw the graph of $2x + y = 10$.

(a) First copy this table of values.

x	0	1	2	3	4	5
y						

(b) When x is 0, we get $2 \times 0 + y = 10$.
What must y be? Put it in your table.

(c) When x is 1, we get $2 \times 1 + y = 10$,
so $2 + y = 10$. What is y? Put the value of y in the table.

(d) In the same way, work out what y is when x is 2,
then 3, 4 and 5 and put them in the table.

(e) On graph paper, draw axes with both x and y going from 0 to 10.
Plot the points from the table. Draw and label the line $2x + y = 10$.

(f) From the graph, what is y when $x = 3.5$?

(g) What is x when $y = 7$?

E4 On a copy of this diagram,
draw and label the following lines.

$y = 2x$ and $x + y = 5$

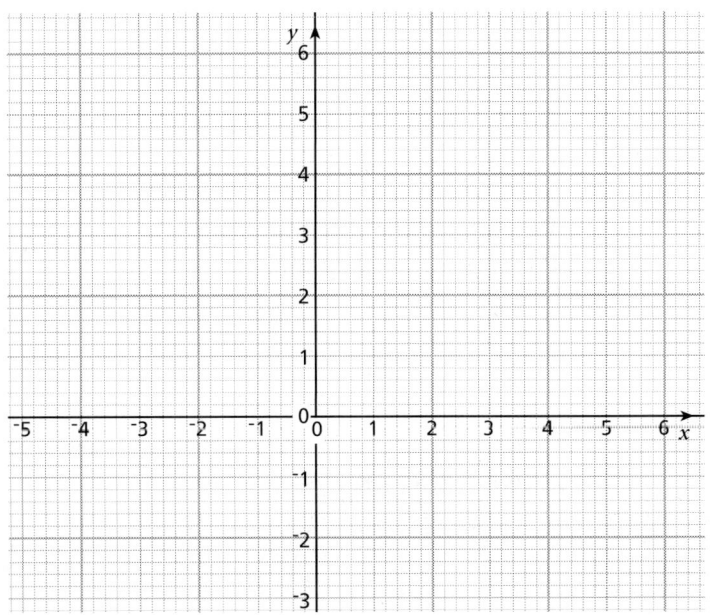

AQA(SEG) 1998

*E5 To draw the line with rule $2x + 3y = 24$

(a) Copy the table.

(b) Check that $x = 0$, $y = 8$ fits the rule.

(c) Check that $x = 3$, $y = 6$ fits.

x	0	3	6	9	12
y	8	6			

(d) When $x = 6$, the rule is $2 \times 6 + 3y = 24$.
So $2 + 3y = 24$. What is y? Put it in your table.

(e) Find the other values of y and put them in the table.

(f) Draw axes with x and y going from 0 to 12.
Draw and label the line $2x + 3y = 24$.

Test yourself with these questions

T1 Look at the numbers in the table. Which of the rules below fits?

x-coordinate (x)	1	2	3	4	5	6
y-coordinate (y)	5	6	7	8	9	10

$y = 5$ $x = 1$ $y = x + 4$ $y = 5x$ $y = 1$

T2 On sheet P113, complete the table for the formula $y = 5x$.
Then draw and label the line $y = 5x$ on the graph.
Write down the value of x when $y = 18$.

T3 (a) Write the coordinates of a point that is on the line $y = x + 1$.
(b) Draw the line $y = x + 1$ on the axes on sheet P114.   AQA(SEG) 1998

T4 (a) Use the formula $y = 2x - 1$ to complete the table on sheet P114.
(b) Use your table of values to draw the graph of $y = 2x - 1$ on the sheet.
(c) Use your graph to find the value of x when $y = 2.5$.   AQA(SEG) 2000 Specimen

T5 Write down the equation of each of the lines in this diagram.

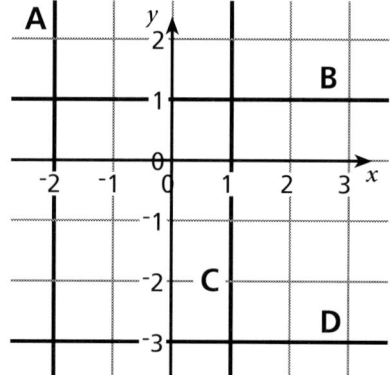

T6 Use the grid on sheet P115 to answer this question.
(a) Draw the line $y = 1$ on the grid.
(b) The line $y = x + 2$ crosses the line $y = 1$ at P.
Find the coordinates of P.   AQA 2003 Specimen

T7 For the rule $3x + y = 12$
(a) Find the value of y when $x = 2$.
Put it in the table on sheet P115.
(b) Complete the rest of the table.
(c) On the grid below the table, draw and label the line $3x + y = 12$.
(d) From the graph, write down the value of x when $y = 4$.

2 Calculating with decimals 1

You will revise
- how to round whole numbers to one significant figure

You will learn
- how to round decimals to one significant figure
- how to find rough estimates by rounding
- how to round off answers to calculations to a number of decimal places

A Rounding to one significant figure: whole numbers

There were **43 576** people at a football match.
The newspaper said

> **40 000 see City humiliated**

The newspaper has rounded to the nearest ten thousand.
The ten thousands figure is the **most significant figure** in 43 576.

Mr Buckfast made **£294 546** from the sale of his software.

> **£300 000 for software!**
> **Mr Buckfast makes a fast buck …**

The most significant figure in 294 546 is the hundred thousands.
The newspaper has rounded the number to **one significant figure**.

A1 Round these numbers to one significant figure.
   (a) 714   (b) 3831   (c) 679   (d) 2052   (e) 77
   (f) 4629   (g) 356   (h) 2481   (i) 8921   (j) 509

A2 Write a headline for each of these stories.
   Round each number to one significant figure.
   (a) 5182 people join a protest march.   (b) 38 426 people attend an open-air concert.

A3 Work out   (a) 20 × 40   (b) 50 × 30   (c) 700 × 20   (d) 40 × 500

A4 Work out a rough estimate for each of these, by rounding the numbers
   to one significant figure. For example, 29 × 53 is roughly 30 × 50 = 1500.
   (a) 37 × 23   (b) 216 × 48   (c) 59 × 72   (d) 32 × 472   (e) 51 × 59
   (f) 196 × 36   (g) 42 × 78   (h) 61 × 326   (i) 56 × 392   (j) 271 × 125

A5 48 people go on a coach trip. They each pay £31.
Estimate roughly the total amount of money they pay.

A6 A concert hall has 288 seats.
Tickets for a concert cost £19. All the tickets are sold.

(a) Estimate roughly the total amount of money paid for the tickets.

(b) Is your estimate bigger or smaller than the exact amount?
How can you tell without working out the exact amount?

B Rounding to one significant figure: decimals

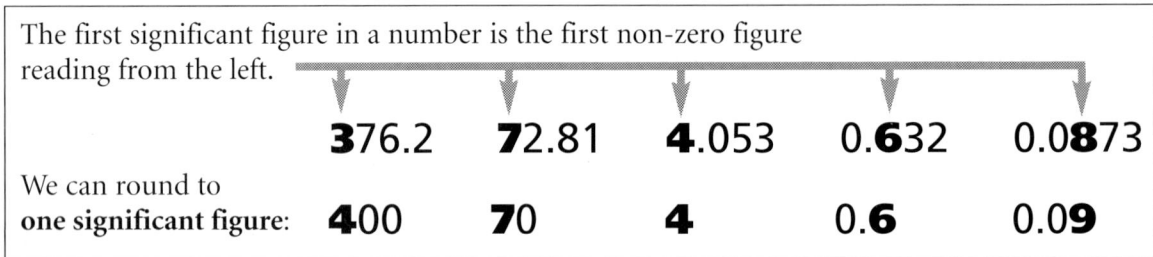

The first significant figure in a number is the first non-zero figure reading from the left.

| | **3**76.2 | **7**2.81 | **4**.053 | 0.**6**32 | 0.0**8**73 |

We can round to one significant figure: **4**00, **7**0, **4**, 0.**6**, 0.0**9**

B1 Round these numbers to one significant figure.

(a) 23.4 (b) 2.34 (c) 67.54 (d) 238.7 (e) 8.717

B2 Round these numbers to one significant figure.

(a) 0.513 (b) 0.762 (c) 0.0432 (d) 0.0685 (e) 0.00473

B3 Round these numbers to one significant figure.

(a) 74.35 (b) 9.204 (c) 0.0613 (d) 173.4 (e) 0.3865

B4 Rewrite each of these sentences, but round the number to one significant figure. The first is done as an example.

(a) The area of the UK is 94 241 square miles.

> The area of the UK is **about 90000** square miles.

(b) The area of Egypt is 386 199 square miles.

(c) An ounce is 28.2495 grams.

(d) A metre is 39.3701 inches.

(e) A cubic foot is 0.02832 cubic metres.

B5 Round these numbers to one significant figure.

(a) 23 476 (b) 0.0607 (c) 7.0053 (d) 346.9 (e) 0.00841

(f) 341 321 (g) 27.953 (h) 247.8 (i) 89.65 (j) 0.1039

*****B6** Round to one significant figure   (a) 983   (b) 0.096   (c) 9921

C *Multiplying decimals*

To find the area of a rectangle, you multiply **length × width**.

This picture shows a square 1 metre by 1 metre.

1 m

1 m

Area 1 m²

The shaded rectangle is 0.3 m by 0.2 m.

Its area is 6 hundredths of a square metre, or **0.06** m².

0.3 m

0.2 m

0.3 × 0.2 = 0.06

Starting with **2 × 3**, you can get to **0.2 × 0.3** like this:

2 × 3   = 6
2 × 0.3 = 0.6
0.2 × 0.3 = 0.06

C1 Rectangle A shows that **0.6 × 0.3 = 0.18**

(a) What does rectangle B show?
(b) What does rectangle C show?
(c) What does rectangle D show?
(d) Work these out.
  (i) 0.6 × 0.4   (ii) 0.5 × 0.6
  (iii) 0.7 × 0.7   (iv) 0.1 × 0.9
  (v) 0.8 × 0.5   (vi) 0.3 × 0.3

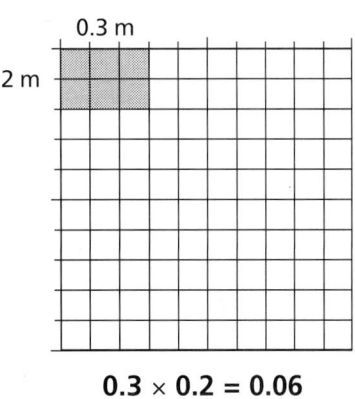

C2 Copy these and fill in the missing numbers.

(a)
5 × 3 = 15
5 × 0.3 = …
0.5 × 0.3 = …

(b)
3 × 7 = 21
3 × 0.7 = …
0.3 × 0.7 = …

(c)
6 × 5 = 30
6 × 0.5 = …
0.6 × 0.5 = …

C3 Work these out

(a) 0.3 × 0.8   (b) 0.7 × 0.1   (c) 0.1 × 0.1

> **The 'decimal places' rule for multiplication**
>
> $$0.\underline{2} \times 0.\underline{3} = 0.\underline{06}$$
>
> There are the same number of decimal places altogether here ... and here.
>
> This rule works for other multiplications:
>
> **A** Count the decimal places in the calculation.
> **B** Ignore decimal points and multiply.
> **C** From the right, count the same number of decimal places.
>
> **Examples**
>
> (a) 2.1 × 0.3
>
> | |
> |---|
> | **A** 2.$\underline{1}$ × 0.$\underline{3}$ (2 decimal places) |
> | **B** 21 × 3 = 63 |
> | **C** 0.$\underline{63}$ |
>
> (b) 1.2 × 0.05
>
> | |
> |---|
> | **A** 1.$\underline{2}$ × 0.$\underline{05}$ (3 d.p.) |
> | **B** 12 × 5 = 60 |
> | **C** 0.$\underline{060}$ |
>
> (c) 30 × 0.5
>
> | |
> |---|
> | **A** 30 × 0.$\underline{5}$ (1 d.p.) |
> | **B** 30 × 5 = 150 |
> | **C** 15.$\underline{0}$ |

C4 (a) Write down the answer to 2 × 11.
 (b) Now write down the answer to each of these.
   (i) 0.2 × 11 (ii) 0.2 × 1.1 (iii) 2 × 0.11 (iv) 0.2 × 0.11 (v) 0.02 × 1.1

C5 (a) Write down the answer to 12 × 3.
 (b) Now write down the answer to each of these.
   (i) 1.2 × 3 (ii) 1.2 × 0.3 (iii) 0.12 × 3 (iv) 0.12 × 0.3 (v) 1.2 × 0.03

C6 (a) Write down the answer to 21 × 4.
 (b) Now write down the answer to each of these.
   (i) 21 × 0.4 (ii) 2.1 × 0.04 (iii) 0.21 × 0.4 (iv) 21 × 0.04 (v) 0.21 × 0.04

C7 You are told that 14 × 23 = 322.
 Write down the answer to each of these.
 (a) 14 × 0.23 (b) 1.4 × 2.3 (c) 0.14 × 2.3 (d) 1.4 × 0.23 (e) 0.14 × 0.23

C8 You are told that 216 × 45 = 9720.
 Write down the answer to each of these.
 (a) 21.6 × 45 (b) 2.16 × 4.5 (c) 216 × 0.45 (d) 2.16 × 0.45 (e) 0.216 × 4.5

C9 Work these out.
 (a) 20 × 0.6 (b) 0.3 × 900 (c) 0.04 × 30 (d) 50 × 0.4 (e) 0.6 × 500
 (f) 0.4 × 30 (g) 0.3 × 400 (h) 300 × 0.6 (i) 80 × 0.5 (j) 0.2 × 0.2

*C10 This diagram shows how you can work out the area of a rectangle 2.6 m by 1.4 m by splitting it into four parts.

(a) Work out the area of each part.

(b) Work out the total area.

	2 m	0.6 m
1 m	A	B
0.4 m	C	D

*C11 Use a similar method to work out 2.3 × 1.2.

D Rough estimates with decimals

Worked example

Work out a rough estimate for 34.8 × 0.572.

Round the numbers to one significant figure.

Rough estimate = 30 × 0.6

30 × 6 = 180
So 30 × 0.6 = 18.0   Estimate: **18**

D1 Work out a rough estimate for each of these.

(a) 21.6 × 0.387 (b) 0.614 × 48.9 (c) 3.882 × 0.187 (d) 48.9 × 0.713

D2 A group of 28 people are going to a concert. Tickets are £19.75 each.

(a) Estimate roughly the total cost of the tickets.

(b) Is your rough estimate bigger or smaller than the exact amount? How can you tell without working out the exact amount?

D3 Sadia bought 38 plants each costing £1.95.
The shop charged her £81.70.
How can you tell, without working out the exact amount, that the shop was wrong?

D4 James is packing textbooks to send to a school.
He has 62 books. Each book weighs 0.51 kg.

(a) Estimate roughly the total weight of the books.

(b) Is your estimate bigger or smaller than the exact total weight? How can you tell?

D5 Work out a rough estimate for each of these.

(a) 7.83 × 0.194 (b) 21.5 × 0.078 (c) 48.83 × 0.389 (d) 217.6 × 0.81
(e) 31.3 × 0.087 (f) 0.894 × 47.8 (g) 61.82 × 0.287 (h) 103.9 × 0.011

Worked example

Work out a rough estimate for $\dfrac{61.4 \times 0.479}{19.3}$.

Round the numbers to one significant figure.

Rough estimate = $\dfrac{60 \times 0.5}{20} = \dfrac{30}{20} = \mathbf{1.5}$

D6 Work out a rough estimate for each of these.

(a) $\dfrac{32.4 \times 0.212}{2.93}$ (b) $\dfrac{79.4 \times 0.269}{3.87}$ (c) $\dfrac{397 \times 0.188}{19.6}$ (d) $\dfrac{0.782 \times 512}{38.2}$

D7 Work out a rough estimate for each of these.

(a) $\dfrac{87.2 \times 0.296}{3.03}$ (b) $\dfrac{0.048 \times 578}{1.88}$ (c) $\dfrac{5879 \times 0.231}{4.12}$ (d) $\dfrac{0.0764 \times 582}{6.15}$

E *Rounding answers*

Rounding to decimal places: worked examples

(a) Round 3.2864 to 2 decimal places.

Stop the number after 2 decimal places: 3.28|64
The next digit is 5 or more, so round up: **3.29**

(b) Round 35.967 to 1 decimal place.

Stop the number after 1 decimal place: 35.9|67
The next digit is 5 or more, so round up: **36.0**

Leave the 0 here.
It shows that the number has been rounded to 1 decimal place.

E1 (a) Round 43.272 to 2 d.p. (b) Round 3.8537 to 1 d.p.
(c) Round 0.74742 to 3 d.p. (d) Round 2.0687 to 2 d.p.
(e) Round 5.2093 to 2 d.p. (f) Round 18.0154 to 1 d.p.

E2 Use a calculator to do 3.46 × 0.873.
Round the answer to 2 decimal places.

E3 Use a calculator to do these.
(a) 0.583 × 43.29, answer to 2 d.p. (b) 10.53 × 3.275, answer to 1 d.p.
(c) 0.274 × 0.076, answer to 2 d.p. (d) 1.483 × 0.0752, answer to 3 d.p.

E4 Daryl buys 29.5 metres of rope costing £3.87 a metre.
(a) Work out a rough estimate of the total cost.
(b) Use a calculator to find the total cost. Round it to the nearest penny.

E5 (a) Work out a rough estimate of the area of this floor in m².
(b) Use a calculator to find the area of the floor. Give your result to 1 decimal place.

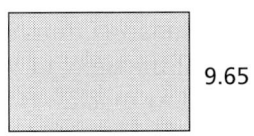

E6 The floor of a doll's house measures 1.16 m by 0.79 m.
(a) Work out a rough estimate for the area of the floor, in m².
(b) Use a calculator to find the area, giving your answer to 2 decimal places.

E7 1 inch = 2.54 centimetres.
Change 36 inches to centimetres.
Give the answer to 1 decimal place.

F Exchange rates

When you go to a foreign country you may need to change money.

Australian money is in Australian dollars (A$).
In June 2001 the **exchange rate** was £1 = A$ 2.10

To change pounds to dollars, multiply by 2.10

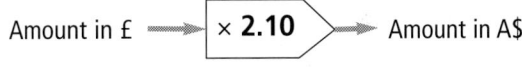

To change dollars to pounds, divide by 2.10

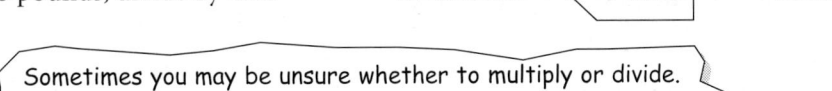

Sometimes you may be unsure whether to multiply or divide. Ask yourself whether the answer will be bigger or smaller.

Give the answers to these questions to 2 decimal places.

F1 In June 2001, £1 was worth 3.20 New Zealand dollars (NZ$).
(a) Change £35 to New Zealand dollars. (b) Change NZ$100 to pounds.

F2 In June 2001, £1 was worth 11.80 Hong Kong dollars (HK$).
(a) Change £52 to Hong Kong dollars. (b) Change HK$350 to pounds.

F3 In June 2001, £1 was worth 1.39 US dollars (US$).
(a) Change £420 to US dollars. (b) Change US$250 to pounds.

F4 (a) Bharat changed £150 into Egyptian pounds (EGP).
The exchange rate was £1 = EGP 1.85.
How much did he get in Egyptian pounds?
(b) In Egypt, Bharat spent EGP 87.40.
He changed the rest of his Egyptian money back into £, at the same exchange rate.
How much did he get?

F5 Paula went on holiday in Singapore and came back with 52 Singapore dollars.
At the time, £1 was worth 2.42 Singapore dollars.
How much was 52 Singapore dollars worth in pounds?

F6 Kate bought a skirt in Thailand for 975 baht.
At the time, £1 was worth 58.85 baht.
How much did the skirt cost in pounds?

F7 Erik had a mixture of English and Norwegian money.
He had £8.50 and 86 Norwegian kroner.
£1 was worth 12.52 Norwegian kroner.

What was Erik's money worth

(a) in Norwegian kroner (b) in pounds

Test yourself with these questions

T1 ESTIMATE the value of $\dfrac{614 \times 27}{88}$

Show clearly how you obtain your answer.
WJEC

T2 Use approximations to estimate the value of $\dfrac{5.9 \times 21.3}{10.2}$.
AQA(SEG) 2000

T3 Work these out.

(a) 50×0.4 (b) 0.4×1.3 (c) 0.2×0.4 (d) 0.03×1.2 (e) 80×0.05

T4 Work out a rough estimate for each of these.

(a) 31.4×0.488 (b) 0.423×69.6 (c) 0.282×0.184 (d) 78.9×0.493

T5 Bhavin went to Switzerland.
He changed £300 into Swiss francs.
The exchange rate was £1 = 2.40 Swiss francs.
Work out the number of Swiss francs Bhavin got.

T6 (a) Susan changed £500 into South African Rand, when the rate of exchange was £1 = 9.90 Rand. How many Rand did she get?

(b) During her holiday Susan spent 4005 Rand.

(i) How many Rand did she have left?

(ii) She changed her remaining Rand into pounds, when the exchange rate was £1 = 10.50 Rand.
How many pounds did she get?
WJEC

3 2D puzzles

You will revise

- the properties of special types of triangles and quadrilaterals
- angle properties around a point, on a line and with parallel lines
- the sum of the angles in a triangle
- how to draw polygons accurately from sketches

You will learn about

- the angles at the centre of a polygon
- the exterior angles of a polygon
- the interior angles of a polygon

A Different shapes

Squaring off

This diagram shows a square divided into two right angled triangles and a parallelogram.

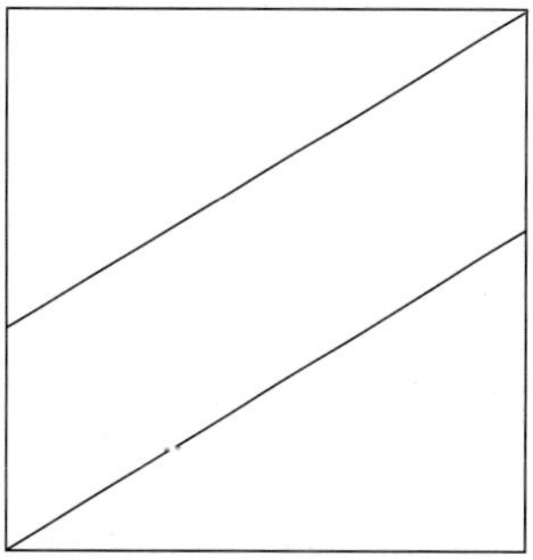

Using straight lines can you divide a square up into

- **A:** 2 right-angled triangles
- **B:** A square and 4 right-angled triangles
- **C:** A kite and 2 congruent right-angled triangles
- **D:** 3 right-angled triangles
- **E:** An isosceles triangle and 2 right-angled triangles
- **F:** 2 trapeziums
- **G:** 2 isosceles triangles and 2 trapeziums
- **H:** A rhombus and 2 arrowheads

Being square

Sheet P116 has two sets of puzzle pieces.

- Describe each of the shapes in the puzzles.
- Describe the symmetry of each shape and any special properties it has.

Each set of pieces can be put together to make a square.
Can you do it?

B Angles in a triangle

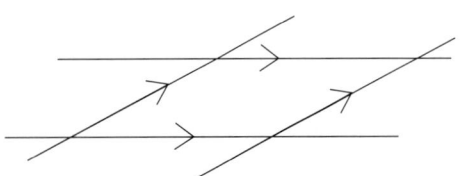
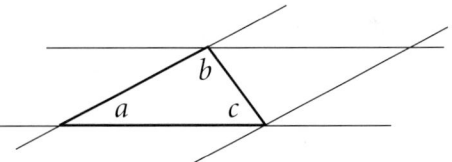

This diagram shows two sets of parallel lines which cross each other.

By joining two opposite corners a triangle can be drawn with angles *a*, *b* and *c*.

- Which other angles on the diagram are the same as *a*, *b* or *c*. Explain how you know this.
- Are there any places where angles make a straight line or go round a point? What does this tell you about angles *a*, *b* and *c*?

B1 Calculate the missing angles in these triangles

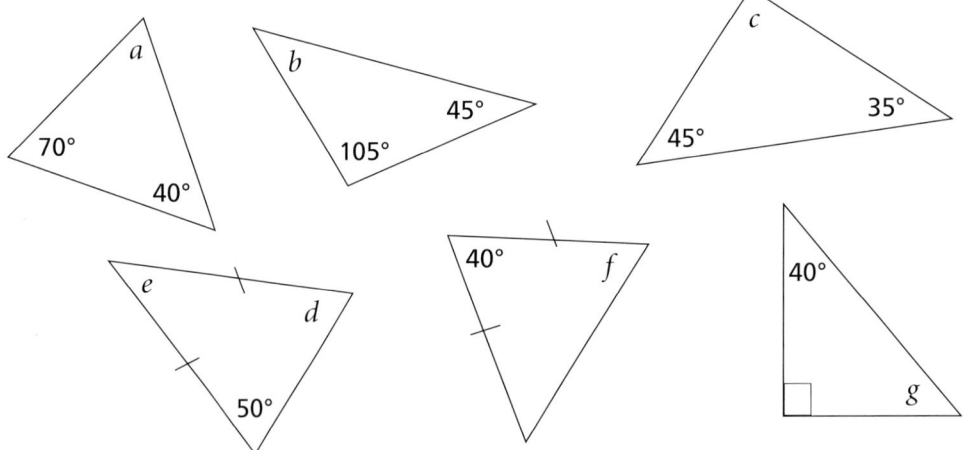

B2 Find the missing angles in this diagram.
Explain how you know using one of the explanations on the right.

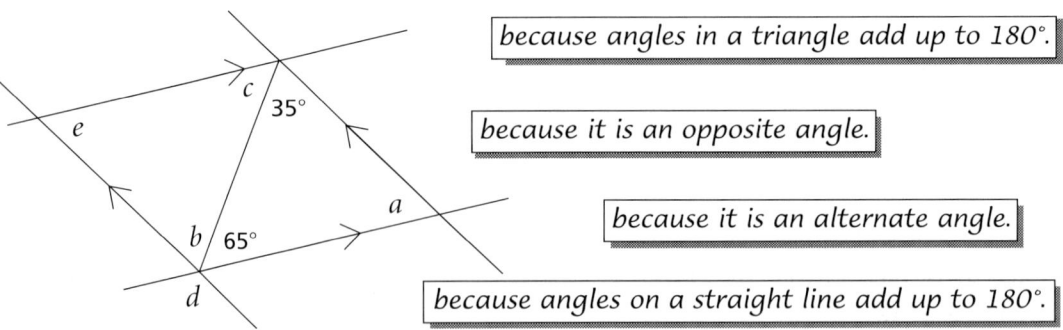

because angles in a triangle add up to 180°.

because it is an opposite angle.

because it is an alternate angle.

because angles on a straight line add up to 180°.

C Angles in a quadrilateral

Here is a diagram of a kite split into triangles.

- What type are the two triangles?
- Can you split a kite into two triangles in a different way?
  What types of triangle are made this time?

On sheet P117 are some other quadrilaterals.

- Write the names underneath each one.
- Split the quadrilaterals to make two triangles.
  What kinds of triangles are made each time?
  Are there different ways? Can any not be split into two triangles?
- If the sum of the angles in each triangle is 180°, what does this tell you about the sum of the angles in a quadrilateral?

C1 Find the missing angles in these quadrilaterals.

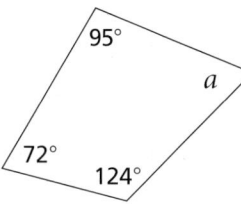
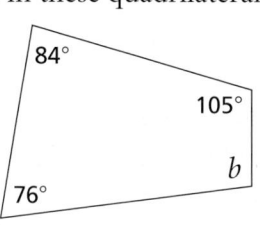
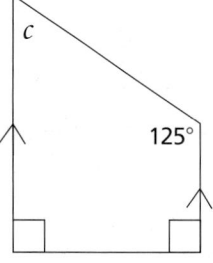
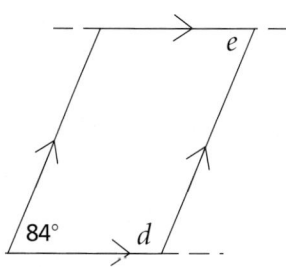

C2 This diagram shows a kite.

(a) What is angle f?
    Explain how you know.
(b) Calculate angle g.

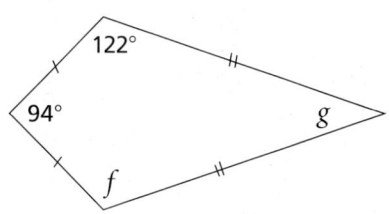

C3 In the diagram lines RS and TU are parallel.

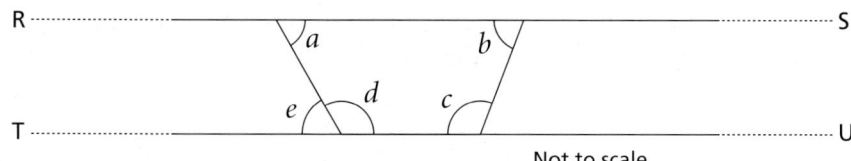

Not to scale

(a) What is the sum of the angles marked a, b, c and d?
(b) Angle $a = 67°$ and $c = 115°$.
   (i) What is the size of angle e?
   (ii) What is the size of angle b?

AQA(SEG) 1998

D At the centre

Here is a simple way to draw a regular hexagon inside a circle.

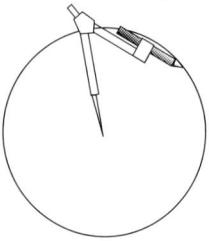 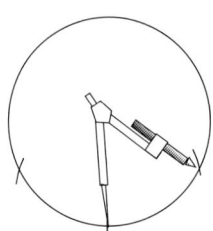 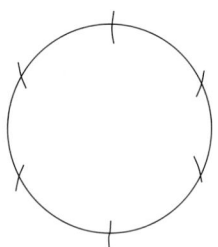 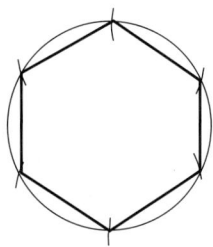

Draw a circle of radius 6 cm.

Mark a point on the circle and two spaced 6 cm each side.

Repeat to give 6 equally spaced marks.

Join the marks up to make a hexagon.

Join the corners of the hexagon to the centre.
How many of these angles are there at the centre?
What must the sum of these be?
So how big are each of the angles?
Check by measuring.

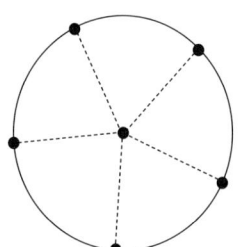

D1 To draw a regular pentagon there would need to be 5 points equally spaced around a circle.

(a) If there were lines from the points to the centre of the circle, how many angles would be at the centre?

(b) What must these angles add up to?

(c) Work out the size of one angle at the centre.

(d) Use your result to draw a regular pentagon.

D2 Work out the angles at the centre needed for the regular polygons in this table.
Copy and complete the table.

Regular polygon	Hexagon	Pentagon	Octagon	Decagon	Dodecagon
Number of sides	6	5	8	10	12
Angle at the centre					

D3 Use your table in D2 to draw each of the regular polygons inside a 6 cm radius circle.
Use an angle measurer to draw the angles at the centre.

A tangled web

These patterns are made from a pentagon and a decagon.

A line is drawn from each corner to every other corner.

Make some patterns of your own like these.

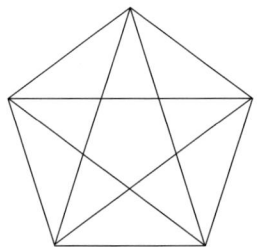 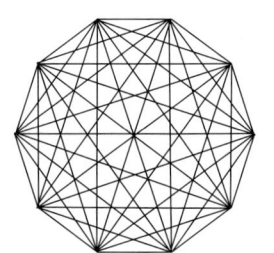

E Exterior angles

If you extend a side of a polygon an **exterior** angle is made.

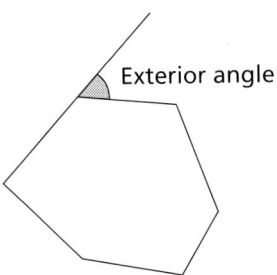

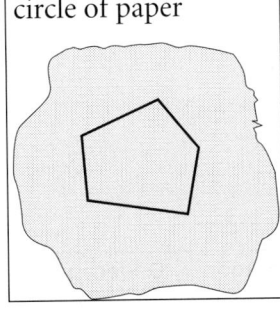
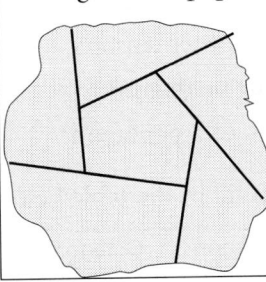
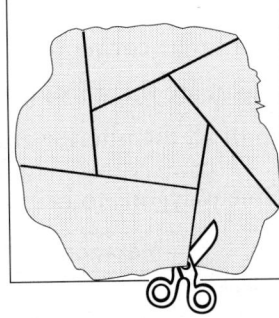
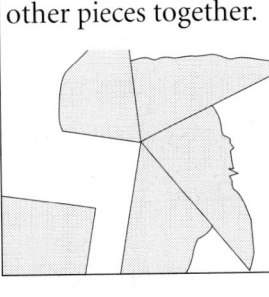

- What happens?
- Can you explain why this is true?
- Will this work for a polygon with any number of sides?

E1 Find the missing angles.

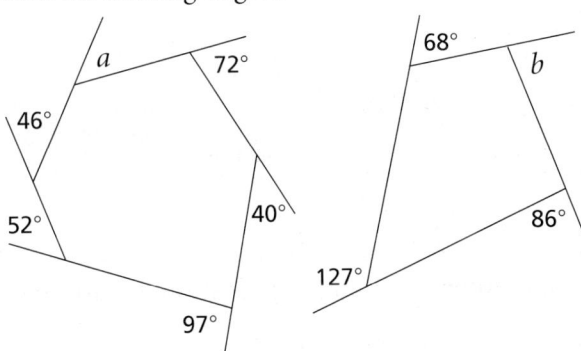
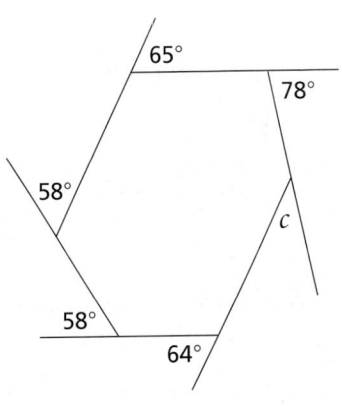

E2 This diagram shows a regular hexagon.

(a) How many exterior angles are there around this shape?

(b) What must the size of **one** exterior angle be?

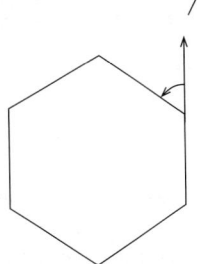

E3 Find the size of an exterior angle on

(a) a pentagon   (b) octagon.

F Interior angles

This hexagon has been split into 4 triangles
by cutting from one corner to another corner.

- Are there other ways the hexagon could
  be cut from one corner to the other to make triangles?
- What does this tell you about the sum
  of the angles in this hexagon?
- Draw a hexagon of your own.
  How many triangles can this be split into by cutting from one corner to each other one?

F1 (a) Draw a pentagon with a ruler – it does not have to be regular.
Draw lines from a single corner to all the other corners.

(b) How many triangles are there inside your pentagon?

(c) What is the sum of all the interior angles of a pentagon?

F2 (a) Draw some simple polygons to help you fill in the table below.

Polygon	Hexagon	Pentagon	Octagon	Decagon	Dodecagon
Number of triangles					
Sum of interior angles					

(b) Which of these rules in words describes the number of triangles that can be drawn inside a polygon if lines are drawn from one corner to all the other corners?

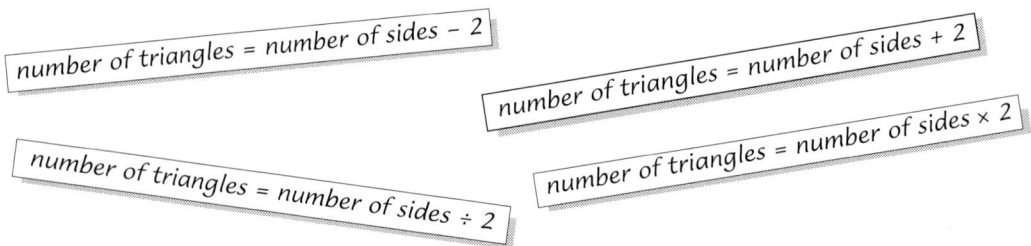

(c) Which of these rules describes the number of triangles (t) that can be drawn inside a polygon with n sides?

$t = n + 2$ $t = n - 2$ $t = 2 - n$ $t = 2n$ $t = \frac{1}{2}n$

F3 (a) How many triangles would be made by drawing lines from one corner to every other corner in a heptagon (7 sides)?

(b) What is the sum of all the angles in a heptagon?

F4 (a) How many triangles would be made by drawing lines from one corner to every other corner in an icosagon (20 sides)?

(b) What is the sum of all the angles in an icosagon?

F5 This shape is a **regular** hexagon.
This means that all the sides and angles are equal.

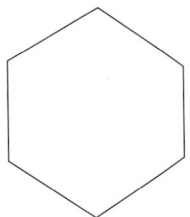

(a) What is the sum of the interior angles of any hexagon?

(b) What is the interior angle of a regular hexagon.

F6 Copy and complete this table showing the interior angle for some regular polygons.

Polygon	Hexagon	Pentagon	Octagon	Decagon	Dodecagon
Sum of interior angles					
Interior of a regular					

F7 (a) Three hexagons can fit exactly round a point. Using your answer to question F5 explain why this is so.

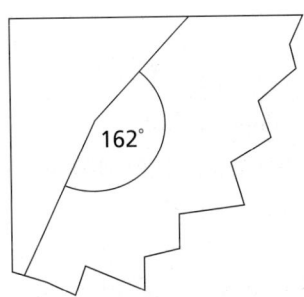

(b) Which of these combinations of shapes will fit exactly round a point

   (i) three regular octagons

   (ii) six equilateral triangles

   (iii) two regular octagons and a square

   (iv) four regular pentagons

   (v) two regular hexagons and two equilateral triangles

F8 (a) The interior angle of a regular icosagon (20 sides) is 162°. What is the exterior angle of a regular icosagon?

(b) Use your results in sections E and F to complete this table:

Regular Polygon	Interior Angle	Exterior Angle	Total
Hexagon			
Pentagon			
Octagon			

(c) Copy and complete this rule:

For any regular polygon the sum of the interior and exterior angle is always ....

G Problems and puzzles

Angles in polygons

Here are some useful facts you should have revised or learned in this unit.

Angles in a triangle

The angles in a triangle always add up to 180°.
The angles in an equilateral triangle are all 60°.
Two angles in an isosceles triangle are always the same.

Angles in a quadrilateral

The angles in a quadrilateral always add up to 360°.
Parallelograms and rhombuses have two pairs of equal angles.
A kite has one pair of equal angles.

Angles in a polygon

The **exterior** angles of any polygon always add up to 360°.
The **interior** angles of a polygon with n sides always add up to $(n-2) \times 180°$.

The angles from the centre of a **regular** polygon with n sides are all $360 \div n$.
The exterior angles of a **regular** polygon with n sides are all $360 \div n$.
The interior angles of a **regular** polygon with n sides are always $(n-2) \times 180° \div n$.

G1 In the diagram lines AB and CD are parallel.
Length AE = BE.

(a) What special type of triangle is AEB?

(b) Angle AEB is 40°.
Find angle ABE.

(c) What type of quadrilateral is ABDC?

(d) Find angle BDC.
Give a reason for your answer.

(e) How many lines of symmetry does ABDC have?

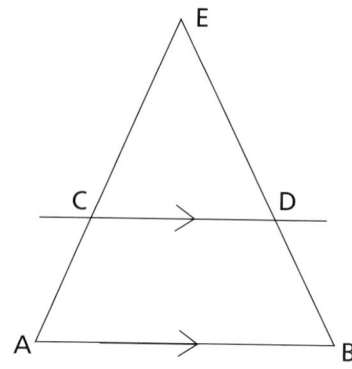

G2 In the diagram two sides of a regular hexagon have been extended to make a triangle ABC.

(a) What is the interior angle of the hexagon?

(b) Work out the angle CAB.

(c) What type of triangle is ABC?
Explain how you know.

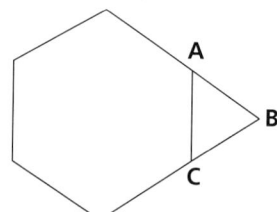

G3 In the diagram lines have been drawn from the centre of a regular pentagon to two of the corners.

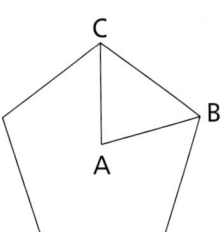

(a) Find the angle CAB at the centre of the pentagon.

(b) What type of triangle is ABC?

(c) Find angle ABC.

(d) Will a regular pentagon tesselate? Give your reason.

Making squares

Make accurate copies of these shapes on plain paper. Colour them in.

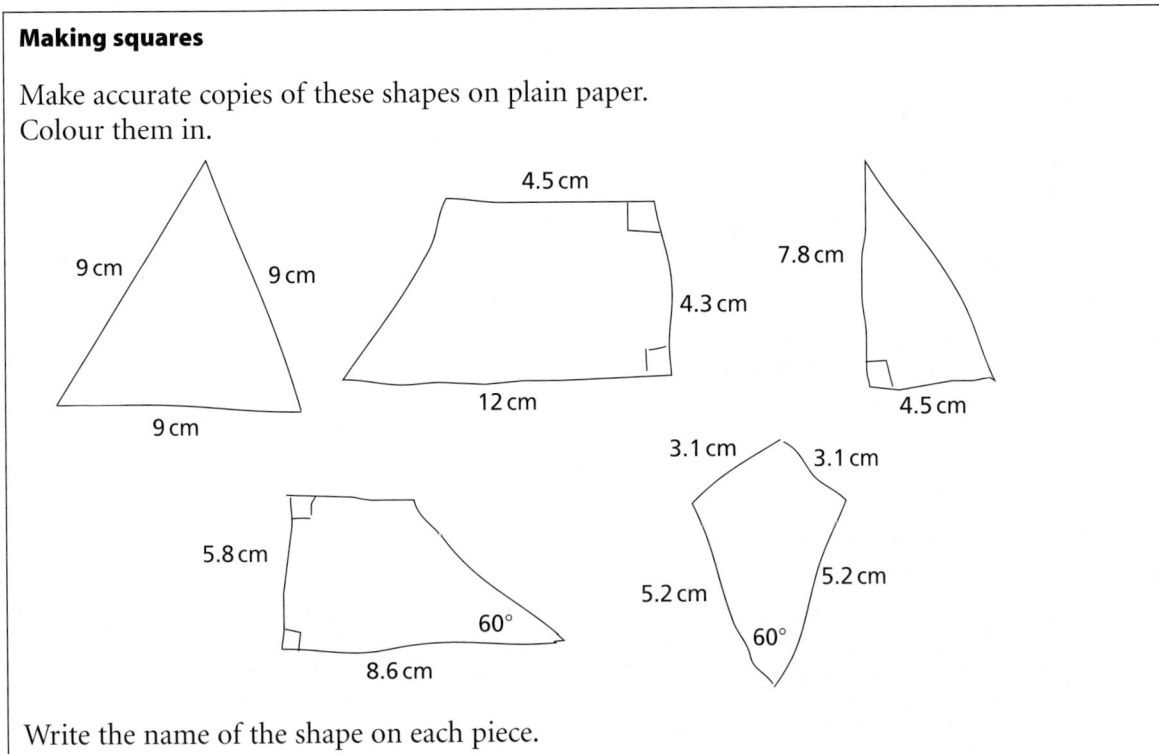

Write the name of the shape on each piece.
Can you put the pieces together to make a square?

Design your own puzzle

Use squared paper to design your own puzzle like the ones in 'Making squares'. The puzzle could be to make a square or some other shape.

Carefully transfer the design to card and cut out the shapes.

Make a sketch of each of your pieces so that someone else could make your puzzle

Test yourself with these questions

T1 Find the missing angles in these shapes.

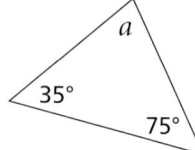 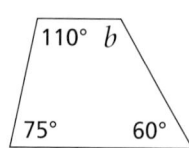 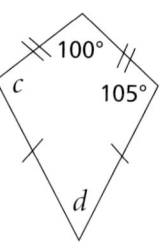

T2 Find the following :
  (a) the sum of the interior angles in a nonagon (9 sides)
  (b) the exterior angle of a regular nonagon
  (c) the interior angle of a regular nonagon

T3 Here is a regular octagon.
The octagon has been divided into six triangles A, B, C, D, E and F.

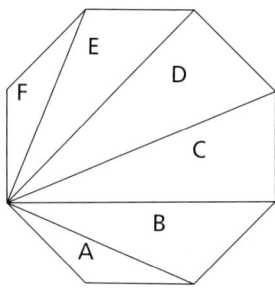

  (a) Write down a triangle that is:
   (i) right angled
   (ii) congruent to triangle E
   (iii) isosceles
  (b) In the octagon, triangles A and B make a quadrilateral.

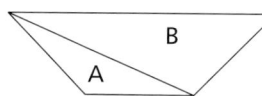

  What is the special name of this quadrilateral?
  (c) Which **two** triangles in the octagon make a kite.
  (d) Regular octagons and squares are used to make a tesselation.

  Calculate the size of the angle marked *x*.

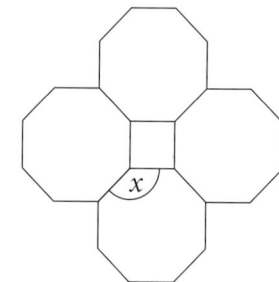

AQA(NEAB) 2000

T4 Two sides of this regular octagon have been extended to make a triangle on one of the sides.
  (a) Find the interior angle of a regular octagon.
  (b) Hence, or otherwise, find the **exterior** angle of a regular octagon.
  (c) What is angle ABC?

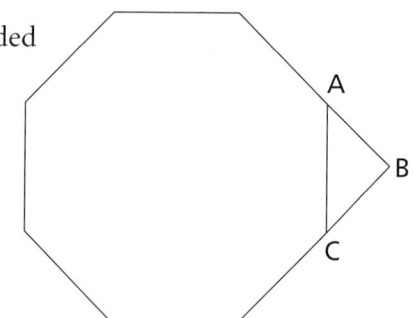

4 Areas of triangles

You will revise
- how to find the areas of rectangles and parallelograms

You will learn
- how to find the area of a triangle
- how to find the area of a shape made from triangles and rectangles

A Review

A1 These shapes have been drawn on centimetre squared paper. Find their areas.

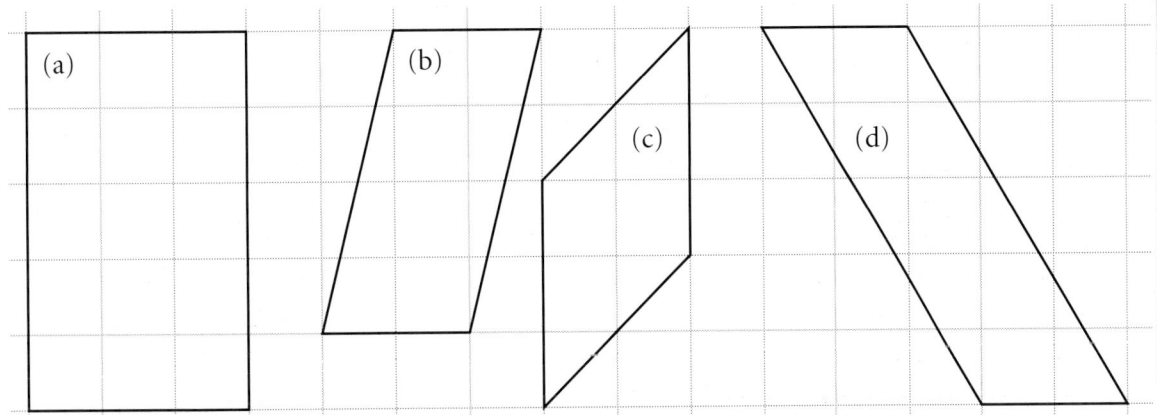

A2 Find the areas of these shapes

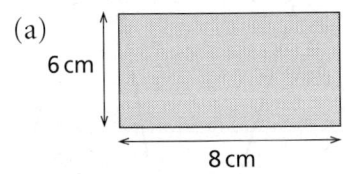
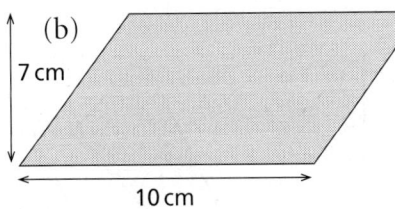
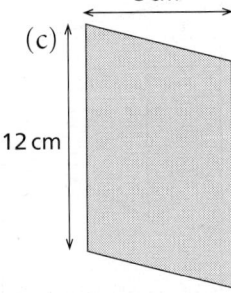

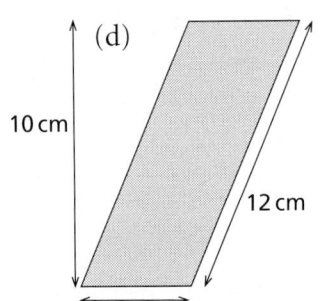
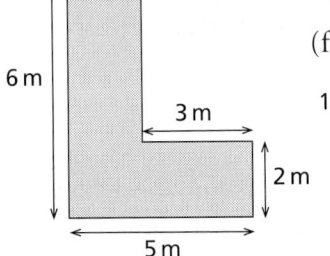
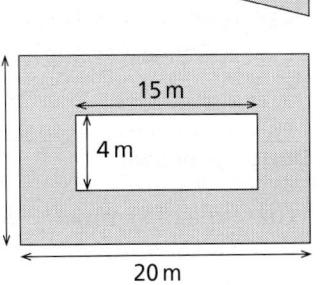

4 Area of a triangle • 31

B Half and half

These shapes are drawn on centimetre squared paper.
What is the area of each of the shaded pieces?

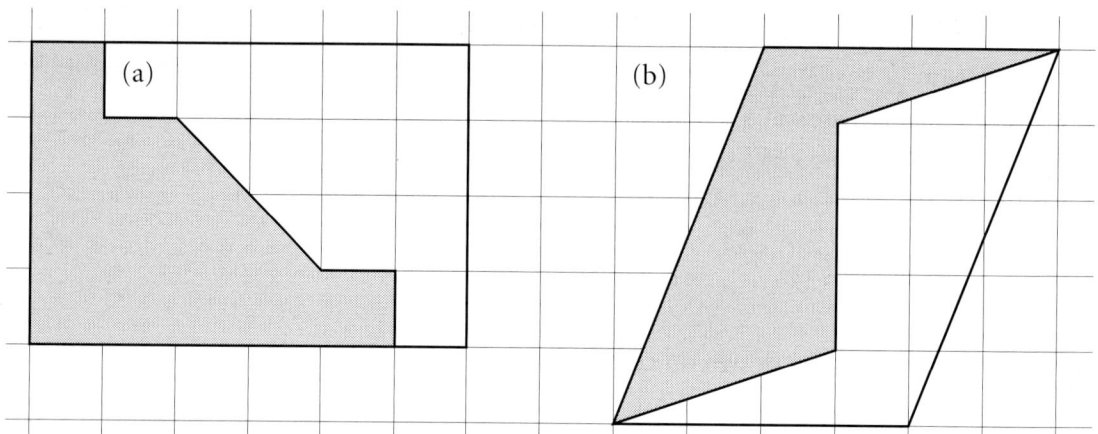

B1 Find the area of each of the shaded shapes below.

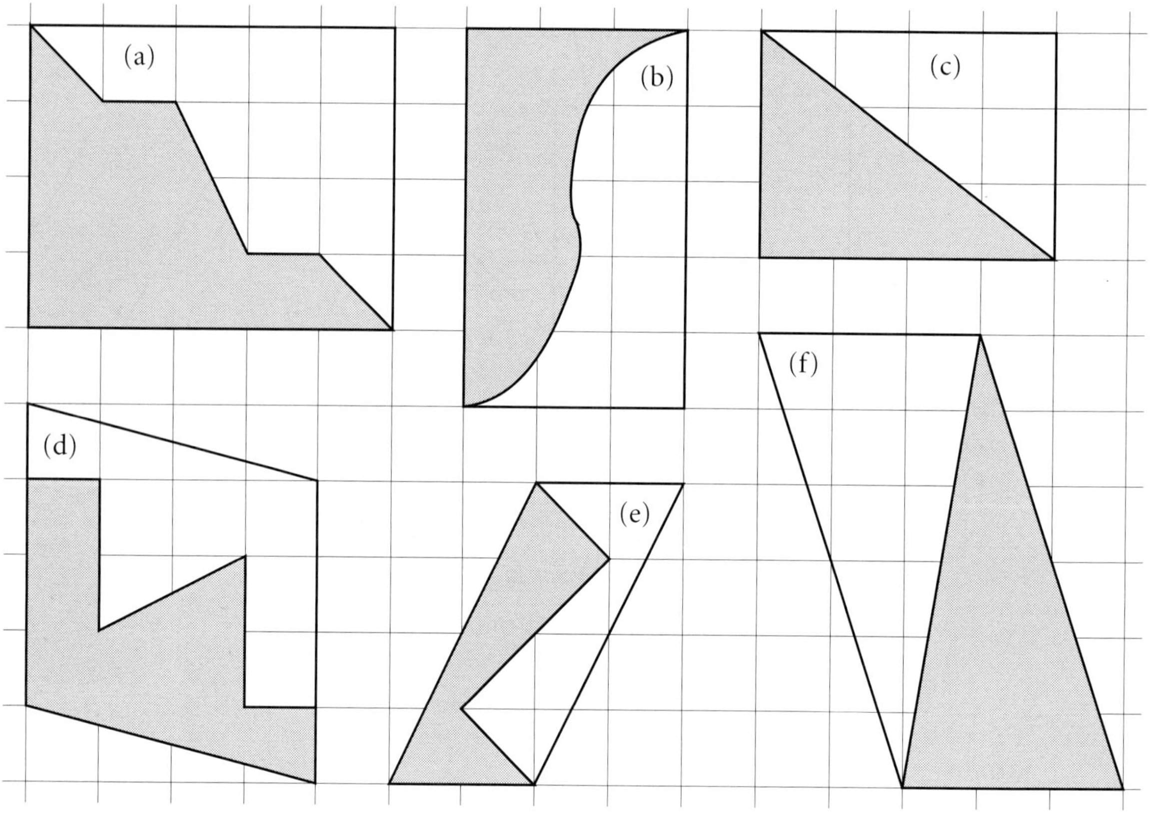

Design your own

What type of symmetry do all the designs above have?
Design a shape of your own on centimetre squared paper that is half of a rectangle or parallelogram.

C Into triangles

Cut out the pairs of triangles on sheet P119.

Can you make a parallelogram from each pair?

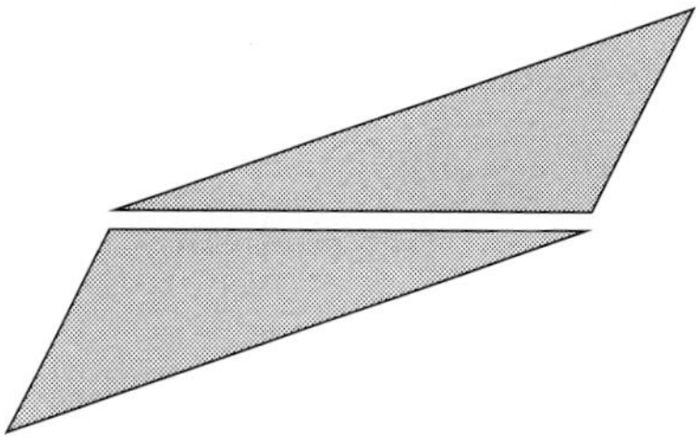

- Put each parallelogram you make on centimetre square paper and find its area.
- Are there different parallelograms you can make with some pairs?
  Do these have a different area?
- How can you find the area of the triangles from this?

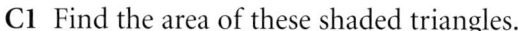

C1 Find the area of these shaded triangles.

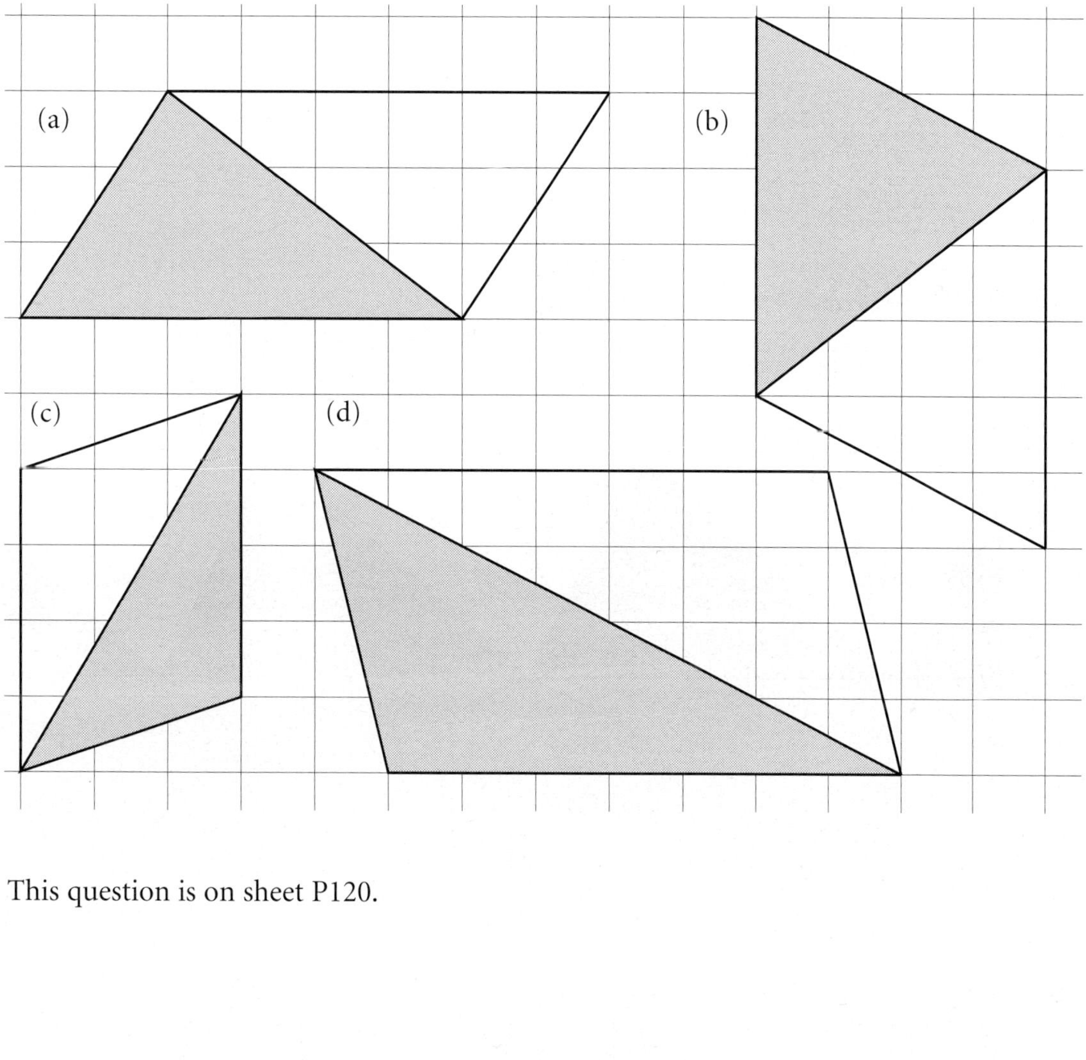

(a) (b) (c) (d)

C2 This question is on sheet P120.

Area of a triangle

Any triangle is exactly half of a parallelogram with the same base and perpendicular height.

The area of a triangle is found by

$$\text{Area} = \tfrac{1}{2} (\text{base length} \times \text{perpendicular height})$$

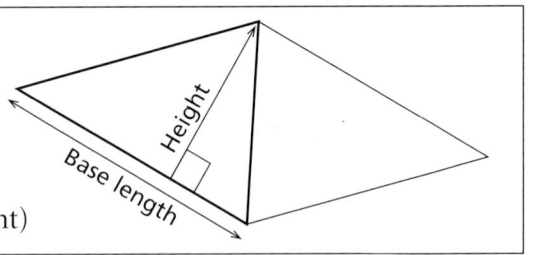

C3 Find the areas of these triangles.
You may not need all the measurements.

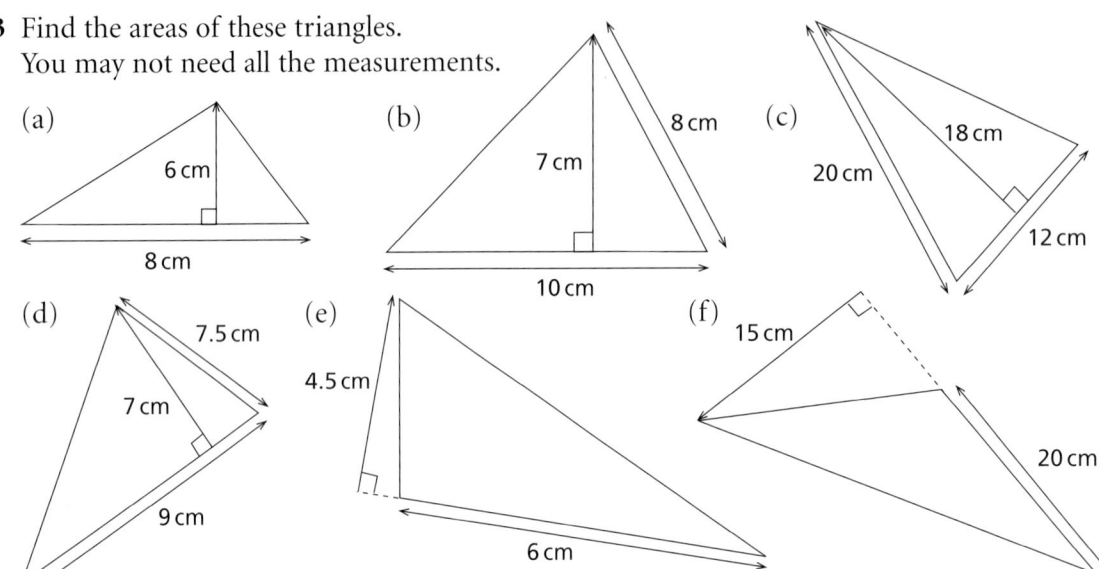

C4 By taking measurements, find the areas of the lettered triangles in this design.

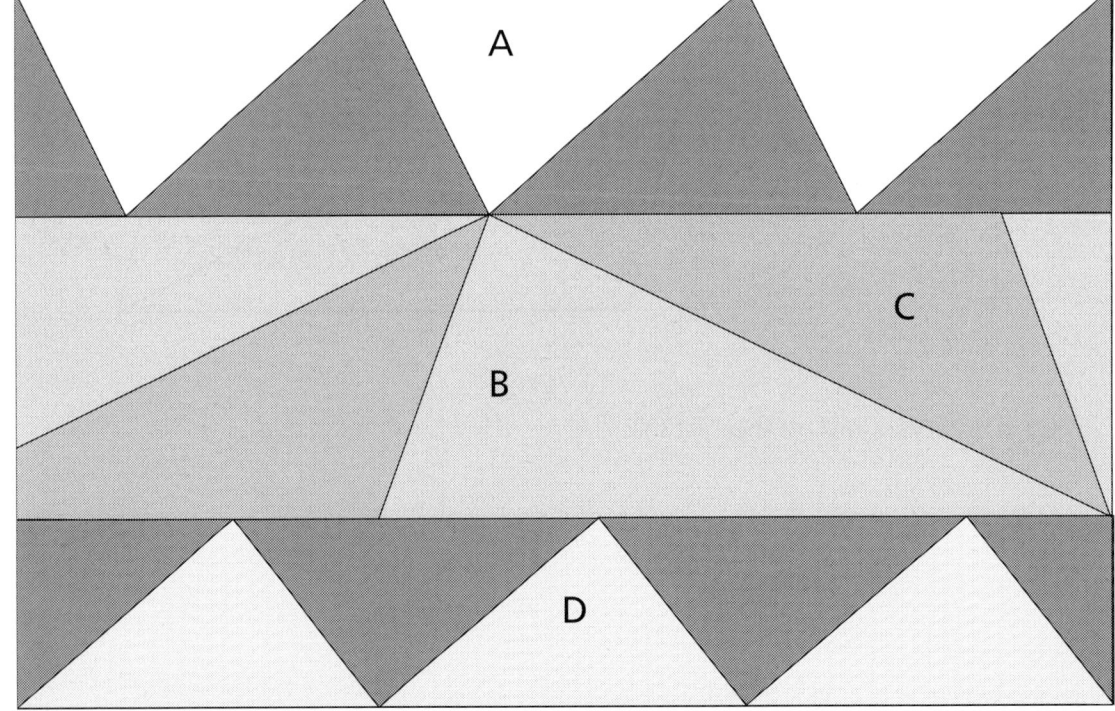

C5 These triangles are drawn on a centimetre squared grid.
Find four pairs of triangles with the same area.

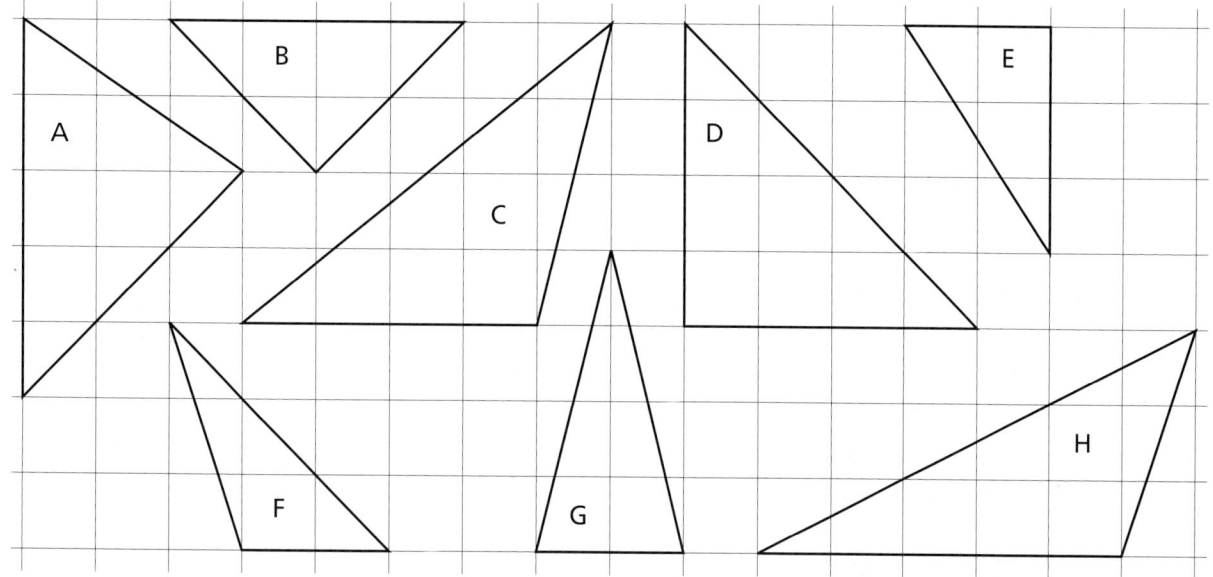

C6 These are pieces of fabric for a tent.
Find the area of each piece in cm².

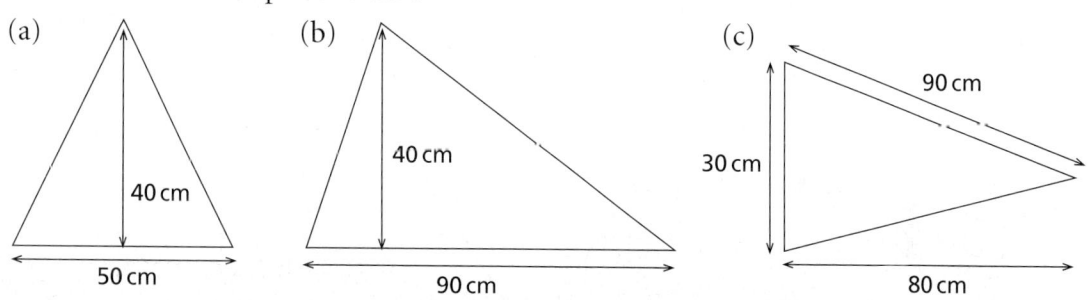

C7 The triangular pieces below are for a stained glass window.
Use a calculator to find the areas of these triangles exactly.

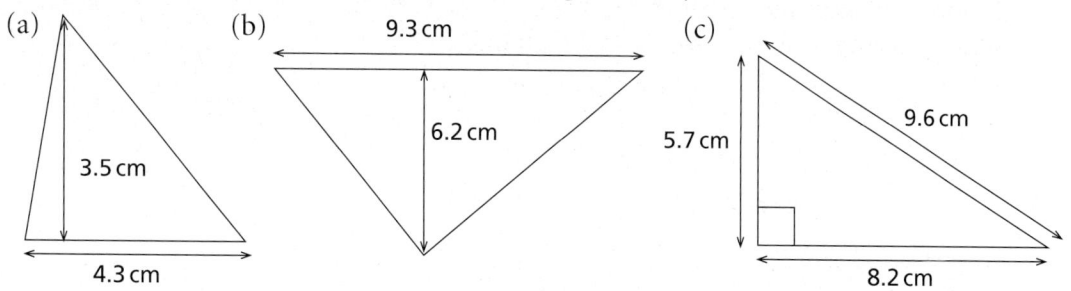

D Composite shapes

Sheet P121 has some triangles and rectangles drawn on a grid.
- Write the area of each shape on the piece.
- Cut each piece out.
- This sketch shows two of the pieces put together to make a trapezium. The area of the trapezium is shown. Find a different pair that make a trapezium. Sketch the pair and find the area of the trapezium.
- Can you fit three pieces together to make a trapezium? Sketch your answer and find the area of the trapezium.
- Can you fit two pieces together to make a kite? Sketch your answer and find the area of the kite.
- Make some other shapes using the pieces. Sketch your shape and find the area.

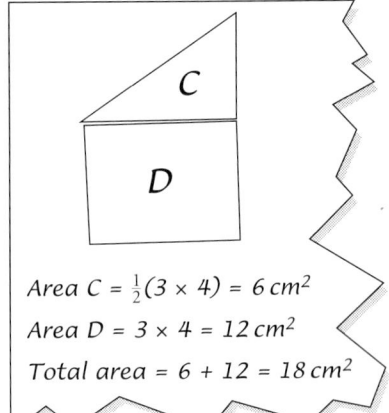

Area C = $\frac{1}{2}(3 \times 4)$ = 6 cm²
Area D = 3 × 4 = 12 cm²
Total area = 6 + 12 = 18 cm²

D1 These shapes are drawn on centimetre squared paper.
Find the area of each shape. Draw a sketch to show how you did it.

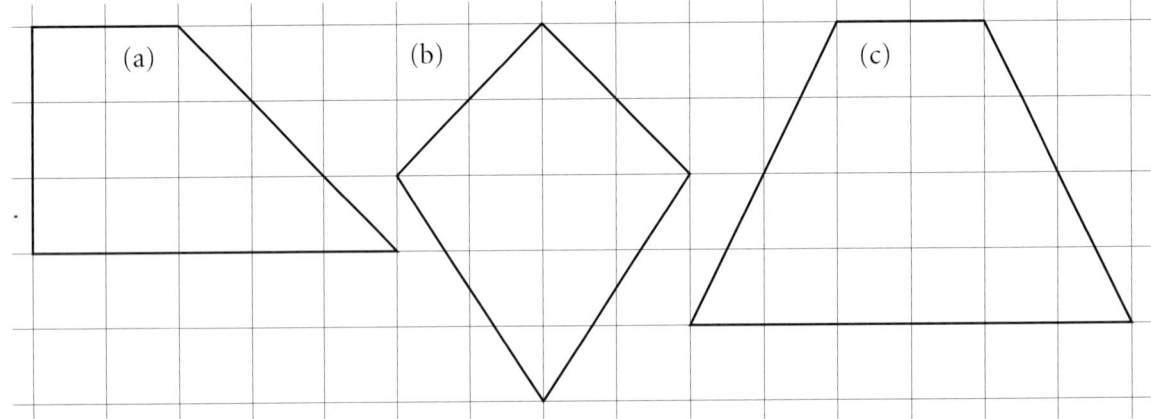

D2 Find the areas of these shapes.
Draw a sketch to show how you did each one.

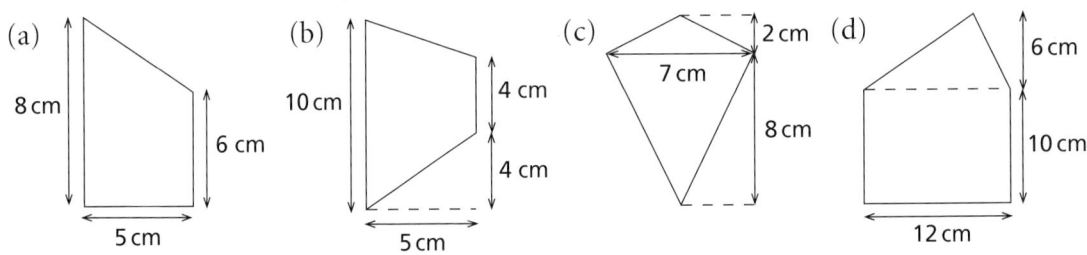

36 • *4 Area of a triangle*

E Converting

This picture shows part of a square measuring 1 metre by 1 metre drawn on a very large piece of centimetre squared paper.

- How many centimetre squares are there along each edge?
- How many centimetre squares are there altogether in one square metre?

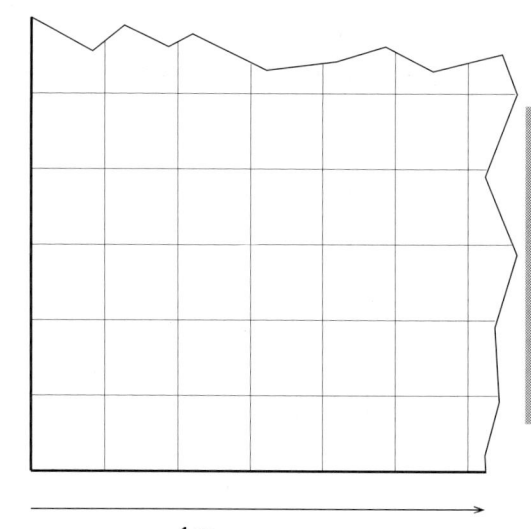

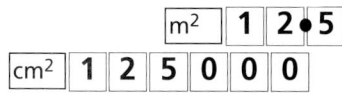

So 12.5 m² = 125 000 cm²

E1 Match up these areas into four pairs of equivalent areas.
Write the answer as a statement, for example 20 000 cm² = 2 m².

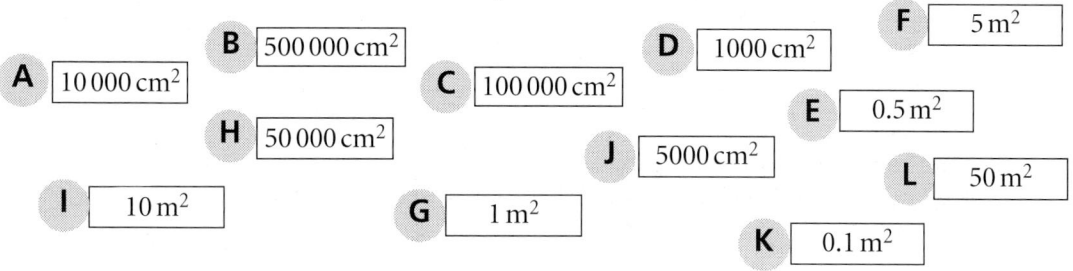

E2 What are these areas in cm²?
- (a) 4 m²
- (b) 20 m²
- (c) 25 m²
- (d) 200 m²
- (e) 2.5 m²
- (f) 4.8 m²
- (g) 0.6 m²
- (h) 0.9 m²
- (i) 0.25 m²
- (j) 0.05 m²

E3 What are these areas in m²?
- (a) 70 000 cm²
- (b) 20 000 cm²
- (c) 150 000 cm²
- (d) 300 000 cm²
- (e) 45 000 cm²
- (f) 85 000 cm²
- (g) 3000 cm²
- (h) 8000 cm²
- (i) 7500 cm²
- (j) 400 cm²

E4 For each of the areas below:
- find the area in cm²
- write down the area in m²

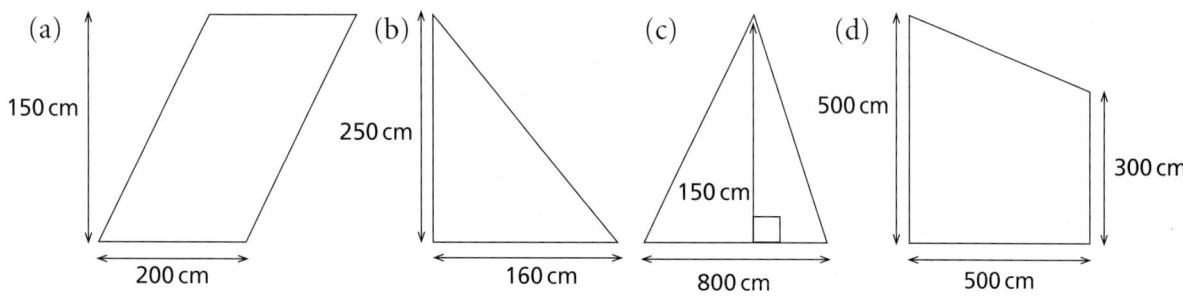

4 Area of a triangle • 37

Test yourself with these questions

T1 Find the areas of these triangles:

(a) 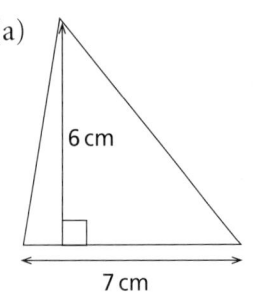 (b) 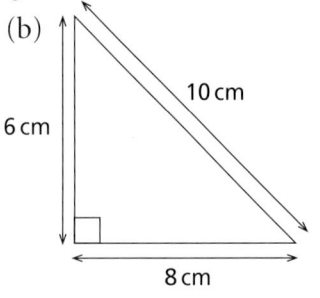 (c)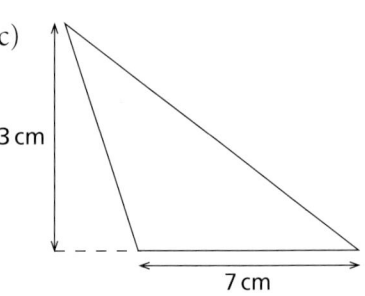

T2 Calculate the area of this flag.

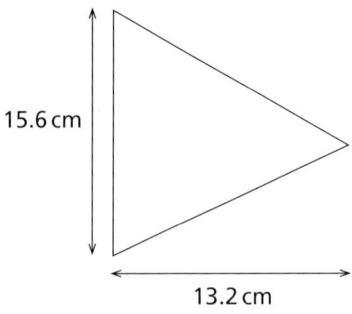

OCR

T3 Find the areas of these shapes.
Use a sketch to show how you worked out your answer.

(a) 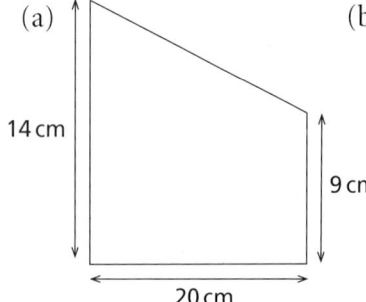 (b) 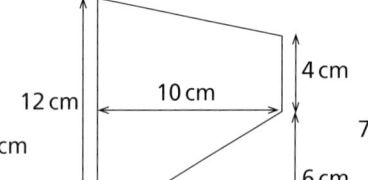 (c)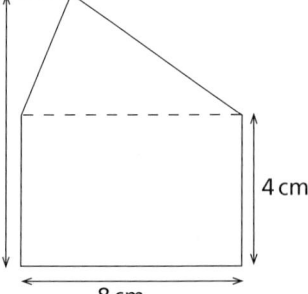

T4 Calculate the areas of each of these shapes.

(a) 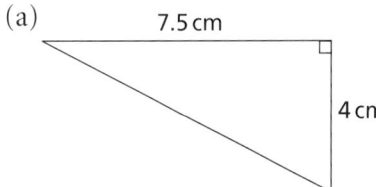 (b)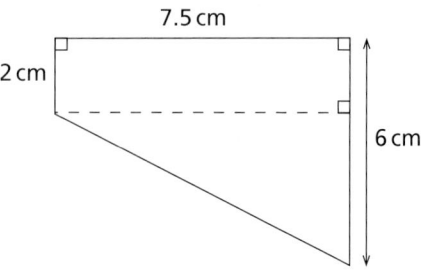

OCR

T5 John has a rectangular patio which measures 400 cm by 300 cm.
  (a) What is the area of the patio in cm^2?
  (b) What is the area of the patio in m^2?

5 Trial and improvement

You should be able to decide when one decimal is larger or smaller than another.
You will
- solve problems by trial and improvement
- work with square and cube numbers

A Searching with your calculator

Missing digits

Find missing digits to make each calculation correct.
- 2■ × 38 = 11■2
- ■3 × 136 = 720■
- 744 ÷ 2■ = ■1
- ■.5 × 3.2 = 2■.2
- 1■5.2 ÷ 24 = 4.■

Rectangles

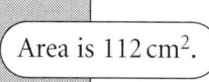

Area is 112 cm².

The length and width of this rectangle are whole numbers.
What could they be?
How many pairs can you find?

Magic triangle

Put 18, 19, 20 and 21 into the circles so that the numbers along each side add to the same total.

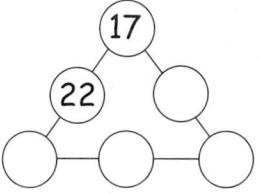

Missing numbers

Find missing numbers to make each calculation correct.
- ▲ × 59 = 1062
- 893 ÷ ♦ = 47
- 71 × ● = 6603
- ▼ ÷ 23 = 41

A1 Find the missing digits to make these calculations correct.
(a) 1■ × 23 = 43■   (b) 9■5 ÷ 39 = ■5   (c) 1.7 × 4.■ = ■.82

A2 Find a pair of whole numbers (larger than 10) that multiply to make 247.

A3 A rectangle has area 210 cm².
The length and width are whole numbers. What could they be?

A4 Find the missing digit to make 5■7 a multiple of 9.

A5 Pat is 3 years older than his sister and their ages add up to 51.
How old is Pat?

B Strips

These are called 'addition strips'.

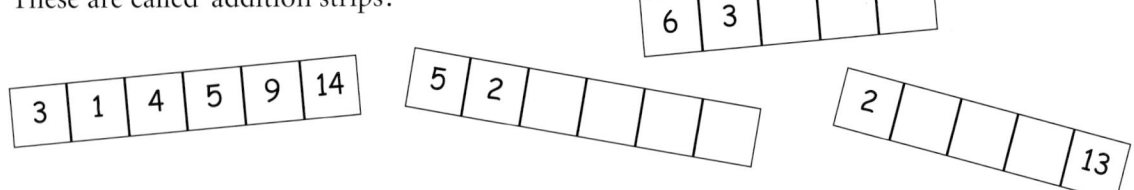

Can you complete the strips?

B1 Copy and complete these addition strips.

(a) 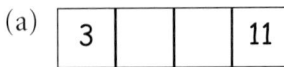   (b)

B2 Copy and complete these addition strips.

(a) | 3 | | | 11 | | (b) | 6 | | | 16 | |

(c) | 9 | | | 24 | | (d) | 4 | | | 29 | |

(e) | 5 | | | 34 | | (f) | 6 | | | 12 | |

B3 Copy and complete these addition strips.

(a) 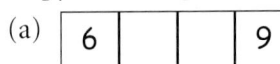   (b)

C Squares and cubes

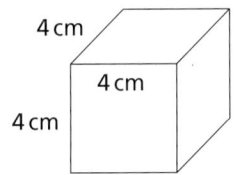

The area of this square = 5^2
$= 5 \times 5$
$= 25\,\text{cm}^2$.

25 is a **square number** or **square**.

The volume of this cube = 4^3
$= 4 \times 4 \times 4$
$= 64\,\text{cm}^2$.

64 is a **cube number** or **cube**.

C1 Which of the calculations below gives the area of this square?

A 3×2 B 3^4 C 3^2 D 3×4

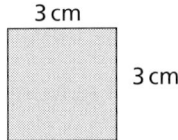

C2 Match these up.

A 2^3 B 3^3 P 9 Q 8

C 4^2 D 8^2 E 3^2 R 16 S 27 T 64

C3 Work these out
(a) 12^2 (b) 6^3 (c) 14^2 (d) 10^3

C4 Which of these are square numbers?
A 100 B 80 C 256 D 441

C5 Find a square number between 200 and 250.

C6 Find two square numbers between 300 and 380.

C7 A cube has a volume of 343 cm³.
How long is each side?

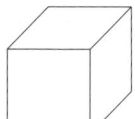

C8 A cube has a volume of 729 cm³.
How long is each side?

C9 Find a cube number between
(a) 100 and 200 (b) 400 and 600 (c) 1200 and 1400

C10 (a) Find n if $n^3 = 1728$ (b) Find x if $x^3 = 8000$

C11 Work these out.
(a) 1.5^3 (b) 0.9^3 (c) 2.1^3 (d) 10.5^3

C12 (a) Find n if $n^3 = 1.728$ (b) Find x if $x^3 = 0.512$

*****C13** Copy and complete the following cross-number puzzle.

Across
1 A square number
3 A square number
5 A square number
6 A square number between 30 and 40
7 A cube number
8 A square number

Down
(Start with this clue.) → 2 A cube number between 4500 and 5000
4 A cube number

D Consecutive number puzzles

> **Consecutive numbers** are whole numbers that are next to each other.
> - 15 and 16 are consecutive numbers
> - 91, 92 and 93 are consecutive numbers
> - 12, 14 and 16 are consecutive **even** numbers
> - 23 and 25 are consecutive **odd** numbers

D1 Find a pair of consecutive numbers that add together to make 185.

D2 Find a pair of consecutive numbers that multiply together to make
 (a) 342 (b) 1722 (c) 650 (d) 7656

D3 Find three consecutive numbers that multiply together to make 2184.

D4 Find three consecutive numbers that multiply together to make 85 140.

D5 Find two consecutive **even** numbers that multiply together to make 3248.

D6 Find two consecutive **odd** numbers that multiply together to make 9999.

D7 Find three consecutive even numbers that add together to make 66.

E Being systematic

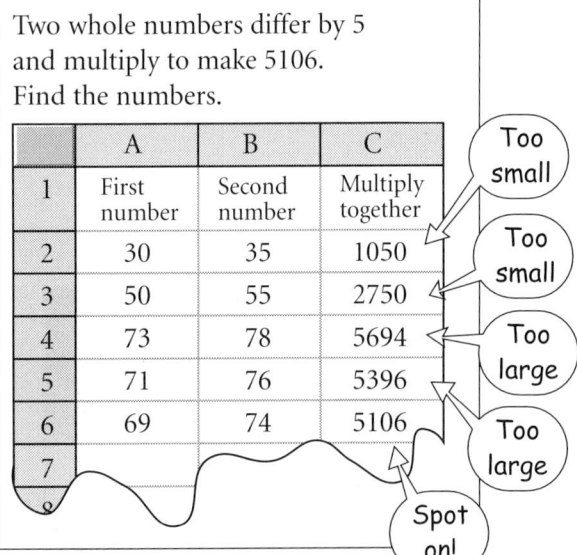

E1 Two whole numbers differ by 3 and multiply to give 2548.
Find the numbers.

42 • *5 Trial and improvement*

E2 Two numbers differ by 0.4 and multiply to make 231.
One number is a whole number.
Find the numbers.

E3 Two numbers differ by 3 and multiply to make 13.75.
Find the numbers.

E4 Two numbers differ by 0.1 and multiply to make 39.06.
Find the numbers.

E5 Two numbers add up to 10 and multiply to make 17.71.
Find the numbers.

F Not exactly

The area of a rectangle is 95 cm².
The length of the rectangle is to be 2 cm more than the width.
Find the width correct to one decimal place.

Width	Width + 2 (length)	Area (target 95 cm²)	Result too small	too large
10	12	120		✔
8	10	80	✔	
9	11	99		✔
8.5	10.5	89.25	✔	
8.7	10.7	93.09	✔	

F1 A rectangle has an area of 40 cm².
Its length is 1 cm more than its width.

Copy and complete this table to find the width correct to one decimal place.

Width	Width + 1 (length)	Area (target 40 cm²)	Result too small	too large
4	5	20	✔	
5				

F2 A rectangle has an area of 650 cm². Its length is 4 times its width.

Copy and complete this table to find the width correct to one decimal place.

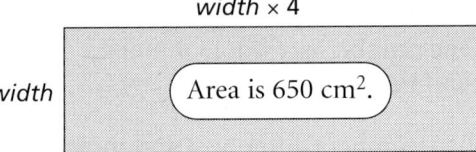

Width	Width × 4 (length)	Area (target 650 cm²)	Result too small	too large
7	28	196	✔	

F3 A cube has a volume of 400 cm³.

Copy and complete this table to find the length of an edge correct to 1 decimal place.

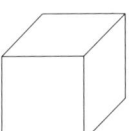

Length of an edge	Volume (target 400cm³)	Result too small	too large
10	1000		✔

F4 A cube has a volume of 20 cm³.

Use trial and improvement to find the length of an edge correct to 1 decimal place.

*F5 Use trial and improvement to solve the equation $x^3 = 50$. Find the solution correct to 1 decimal place.

G Deciding on your own method

Decide on your own method to solve these problems.

G1 When a number is multiplied by itself the answer is 169. What is the number?

G2 Find all the pairs of whole numbers that multiply together to make 663.

G3 A square has an area of 121 cm². What is the length of one side?

G4 What is the missing number in the statement ■ × 13 = 481?

G5 A cube has a volume of 1331 cm³. Find the length of one side.

G6 A square has an area of 150 cm².
What is the length of one side correct to 1 decimal place.

G7 A cube has a volume of 100 cm³.
Find the length of one side correct to 1 decimal place.

Test yourself with these questions

T1 Which numbers in the loop are
(a) square numbers
(b) cube numbers

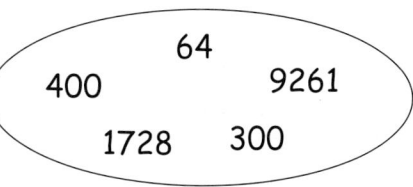

T2 Find a pair of consecutive numbers that multiply together to make 552.

T3 Find two consecutive odd numbers that add to make 76.

T4 Two numbers differ by 5 and multiply to make 2646.
What are the numbers?

T5 Solve this number puzzle using trial and improvement.

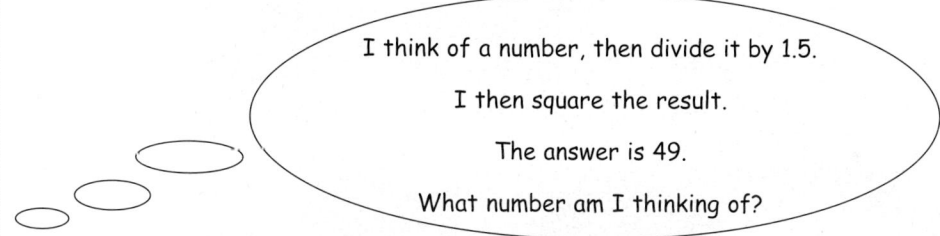

I think of a number, then divide it by 1.5.
I then square the result.
The answer is 49.
What number am I thinking of?

The working has been started for you.
Copy and complete it.

Don't forget to show **all** your working.

Trial	Working out	Result too small	too large
6	6 ÷ 1.5 = 4, 4 × 4 = 16	✔	
12			

OCR(MEG)

T6 A cube has a volume of 75 cm³.
Use trial and improvement to find the length of one side to 1 decimal place.
Show all your trials.

6 3D puzzles

You will revise
- how to draw three dimensional objects
- how to make nets for three dimensional objects
- how to draw equilateral triangles with a pair of compasses

You will learn how to
- show 3D objects in 2D using plans and views
- recognise reflection symmetry in 3D objects

A The Soma Cube

This photograph shows the pieces of a Soma Cube.
The pieces fit together to make a large cube.

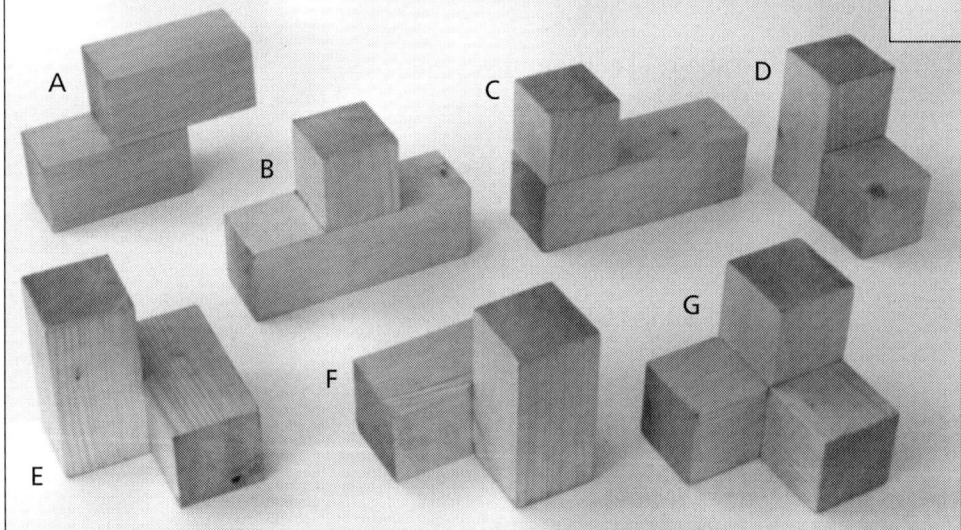

All of the 7 pieces above can be made by sticking together small cubes.

How many cubes are used to make each of these pieces?

Which pieces have the same volume?

Here is piece F, which is made from 4 small cubes.
It is drawn on triangular dotty paper.

- Draw pieces A, D and G on triangular dotty paper.
- Shading sides which face the same direction helps show the object more clearly.

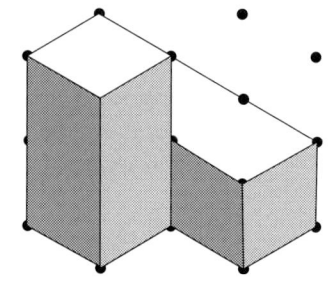

46 • 6 3D puzzles

B Views

Drawing a 3D picture of an object is difficult without triangular dotty paper.

Another way of showing a 3D object on paper is to draw the view or **elevation** from three different directions

- a plan view
- a side view
- a front view

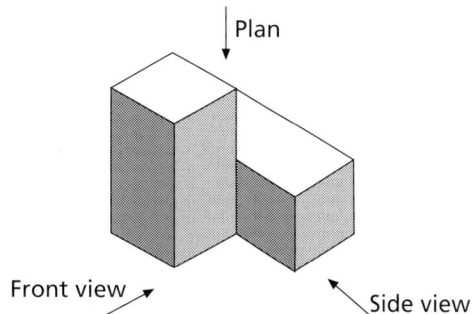

This is a front view of the soma cube piece.

This line is dotted because it is hidden from this view.

B1 Which of these are possible plan views of the Soma Cube piece above?

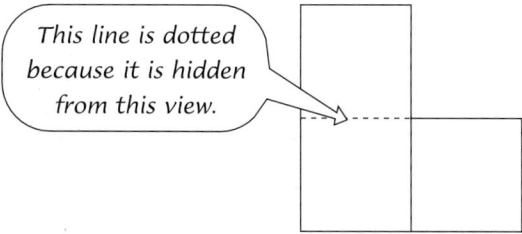

B2 Draw the side view of the soma cube piece above. Make it from multilink if you need.

B3 This is a plan view of one of the Soma Cube pieces.

Which of these is the front view of the piece?

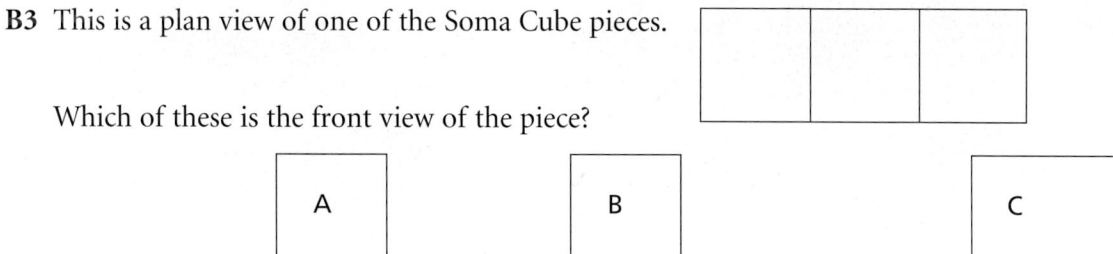

B4 Choose another Soma Cube piece and draw the three views.

6 3D puzzles • 47

B5 This diagram shows a solid object with some measurements.

(a) Which one of the diagrams below is a full scale side view of this object?

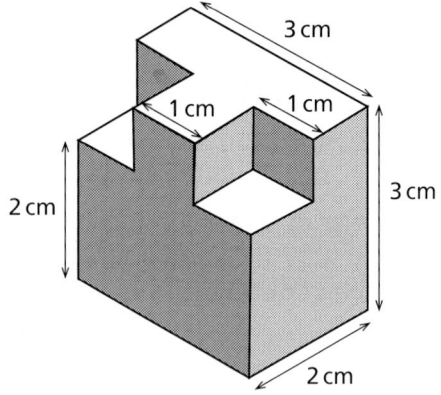

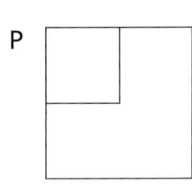 P

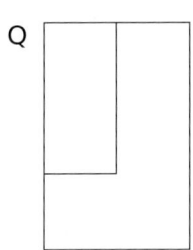 Q

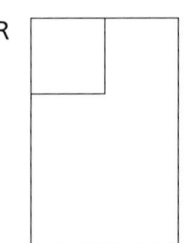 R

 S

Use centimetre squared paper to

(b) draw a full scale plan view of this object.

(c) draw a full scale front view of this object.

B6 These drawings show two views of the same solid made with centimetre cubes. The base of the solid is horizontal.

 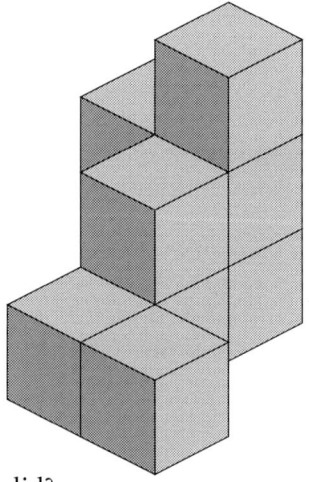

(a) How many centimetre cubes are there in this solid?

(b) Draw an accurate full size plan view of the solid on centimetre squared paper.   OCR

B7 These are views of some everyday objects.
For each object there are two views, which may be front, side or plan.
Identify the objects and sketch the missing view of each one.

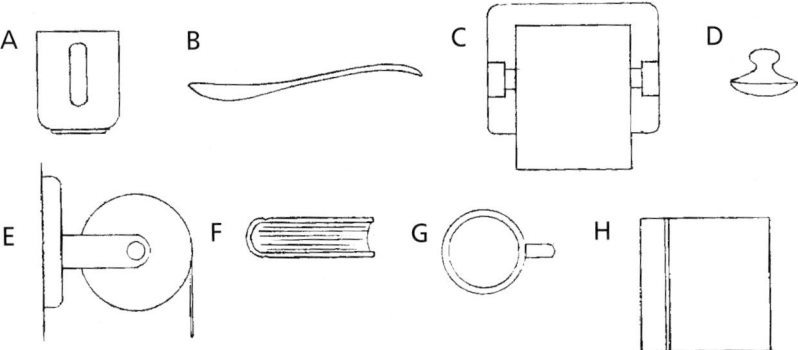

B8 Four views of a model drawing are shown below.

(a) Match each view to one of the directions shown by arrows.

(b) The view from one direction is missing. Draw this view.

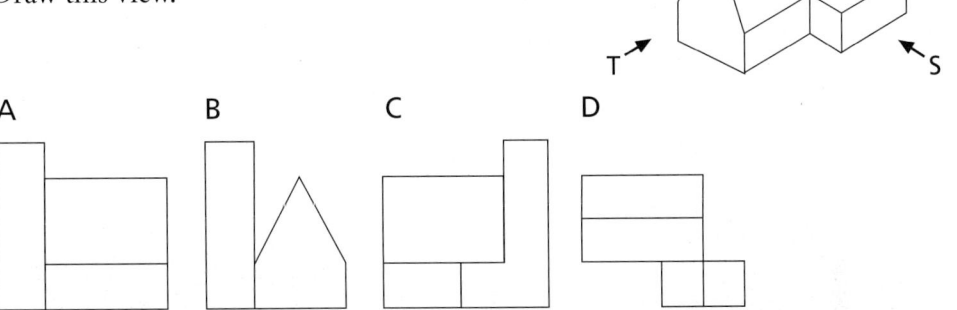

B9 (a) Draw a full size plan view of this shape.

(b) Draw a full size side view of this shape from direction S.
Show any hidden edges with dotted lines.

(c) Use your drawings to measure the length of the sloping edge AB.

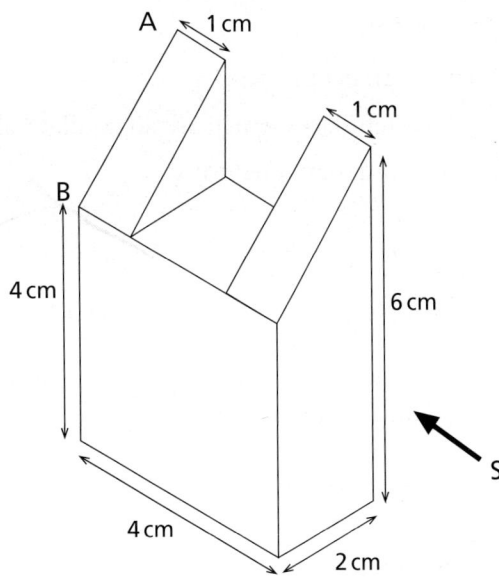

6 3D Puzzles • 49

C Nets

This flat design can be folded together to make a cube.

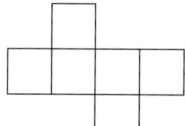
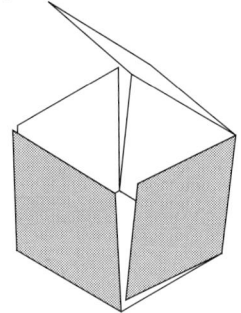

A flat shape which makes up to a 3D shape without overlapping is called a **net**.

Which of these are possible nets for a cube?
Cut them out of squared paper and try if you are not sure.

(a) 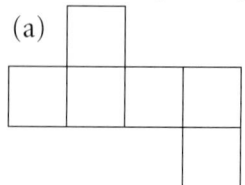   (b) 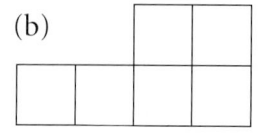   (c)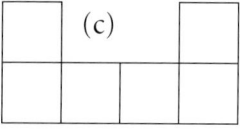

C1 There are 12 possible different nets of a cube.
Draw 4 possible nets of a cube on squared paper.

C2 This is a tetrahedron.
It is made from 4 equilateral triangles
Which of these are nets of a tetrahedron?

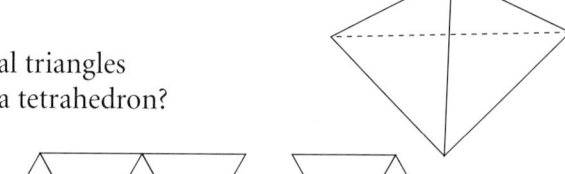

A 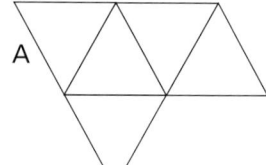   B 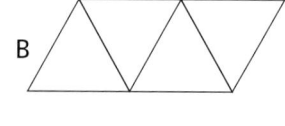   C   D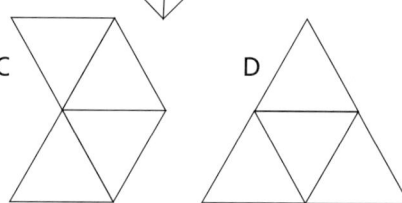

Challenge

This is an octahedron.

It has eight faces which are all equilateral triangles.

Can you design a net for it?

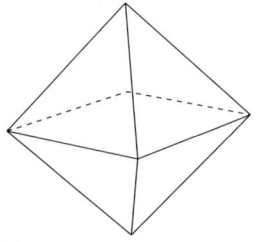

C3 This is a cuboid measuring 4 cm by 6 cm by 8 cm.
Draw an accurate net for this cuboid on centimetre squared paper.

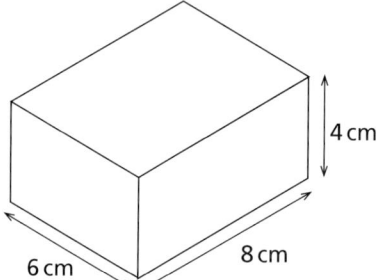

50 • *6 3D puzzles*

C4 The diagram shows a pyramid on a square base.

(a) How many edges does it have?

(b) How many triangular faces does it have?

(c) The length of each edge of the pyramid is 3 cm. Draw a full-size net of this pyramid on sheet P122. (The base has been drawn for you.)

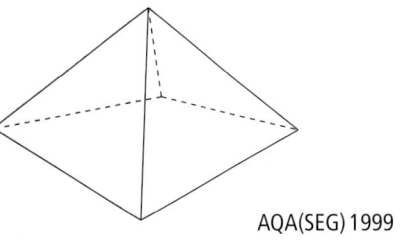

AQA(SEG) 1999

Tetrahedron puzzle

A On a large piece of card, draw lightly an equilateral triangle with sides of 18 cm

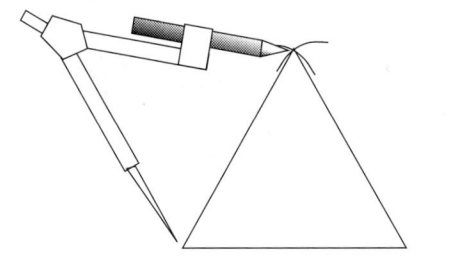

B Mark off 6 cm lengths on each side.

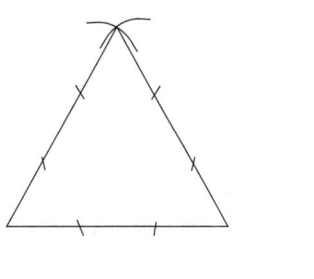

C Add these lines in ink. Rub out all the construction lines

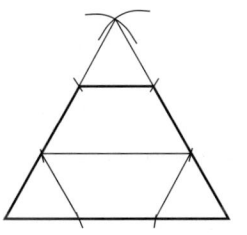

D Add a 6 cm square to the top of the pattern. Add these flaps and your net is complete.

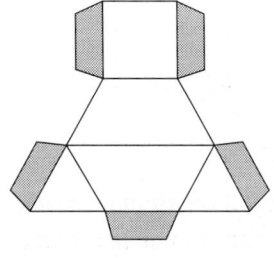

E Make another piece exactly the same, or work with a partner. Try to put the two pieces together to make a tetrahedron.

6 3D Puzzles • 51

D Prisms

These shapes are all prisms.

D1 (a) Which of these objects are prisms?

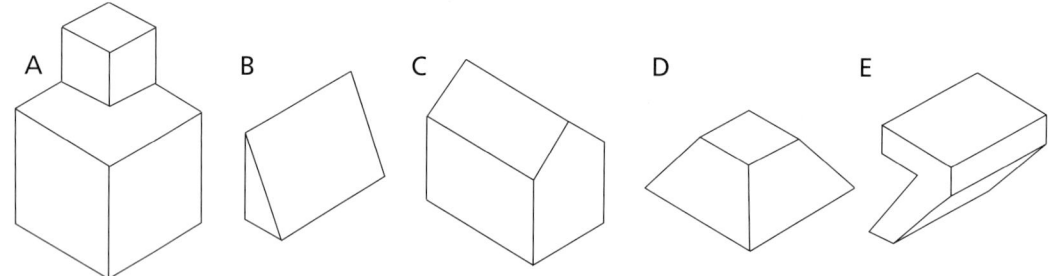

(b) For each of the objects above that is a prism, sketch the cross-section.

D2 This is a triangular prism.
The ends of the prism are equilateral triangles.

(a) Draw a rectangle 10 cm by 5 cm in the middle of a sheet of paper.

(b) Use this rectangle to complete an accurate net for this prism.

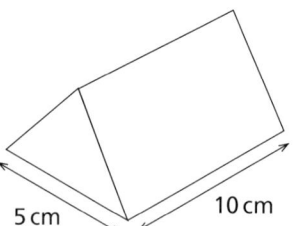

D3 This is a prism with a trapezium cross section.
The front view is drawn full size on sheet P123.
On sheet P123

(a) draw a full size side view of this prism.

(b) draw a full size plan view of this prism.

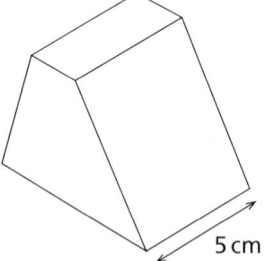

52 • 6 3D puzzles

E Reflection symmetry

Mirror images

This shape is made from 5 multilink cubes.

What would the reflection of this shape in the mirror look like?
Can you make the shape which is the reflection?

Make some different shapes using 5 multilink cubes.
Ask a partner to make the reflection of your shape.
Check that you agree with your partner.

Does it matter where the mirror goes?
Use your shape and your partner's to investigate this.

Are there any shapes where your partner's reflection is identical to your shape?

E1 This shape is made from 5 multilink cubes. Which of the shapes below are a mirror image of this shape?

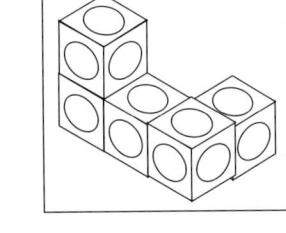

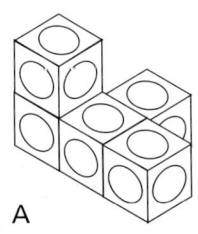 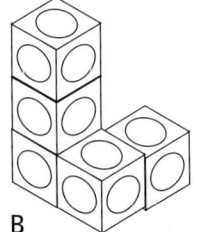 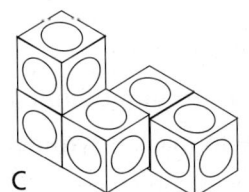 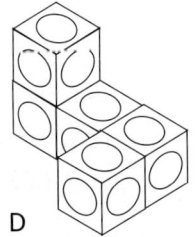

A   B   C   D

E2 Match each of these shapes to its mirror image.

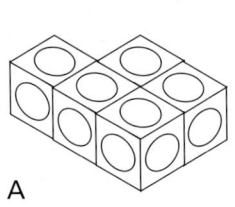 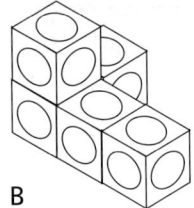 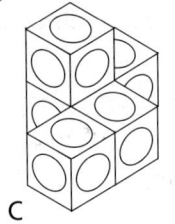 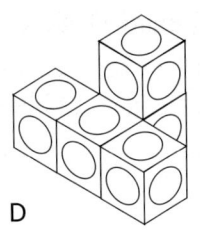

A   B   C   D

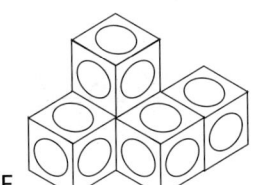 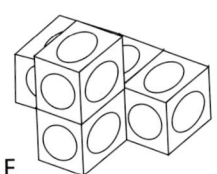 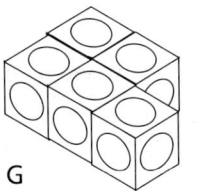 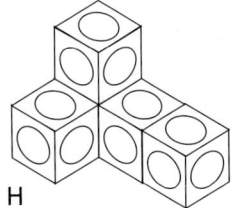

E   F   G   H

6 3D Puzzles • 53

This Soma Cube piece has been cut in half and placed against a mirror.

The reflection makes the piece look whole again This shape has reflection symmetry.

Is there any other way the original piece could be cut in half and placed against a mirror to give the full shape?

A mirror which makes a half shape whole like this is called a **plane of symmetry**.

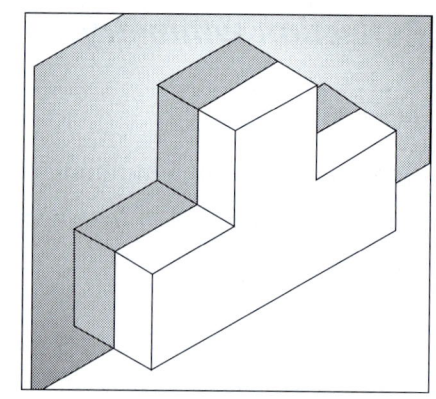

E3 On sheet P124 are some shapes shown cut by a mirror. Draw the other half of the shape.

E4 Which of these Soma Cube pieces has reflection symmetry? How many planes of symmetry does each shape have?

(a) 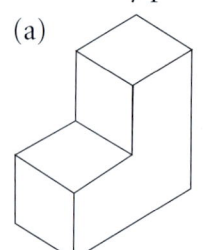 (b) 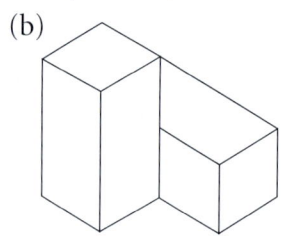 (c) 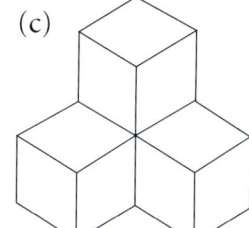 (d)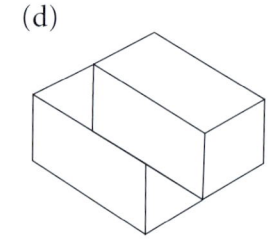

E5 This shape has been made from multilink cubes. It has no planes of symmetry.

(a) Make this shape from multilink cubes.

(b) Add one cube to make it symmetrical.

(c) Sketch your shape on triangular dotty paper.

Make up some puzzles like these to try on a partner.

E6 How many planes of symmetry does each of these shapes have?

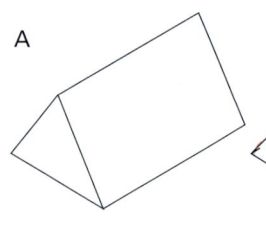 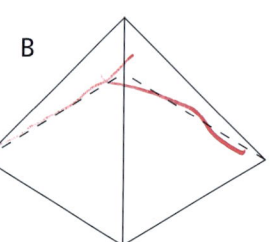 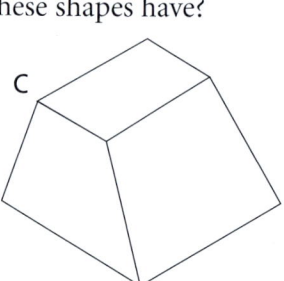 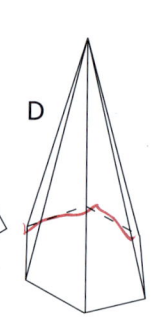

A Equilateral triangle prism

B Square based pyramid

C Trapezium prism

D Regular hexagon based pyramid

54 • 6 3D puzzles

Test yourself with these questions

T1 This diagram shows a box.
Draw a full sized net for this box.

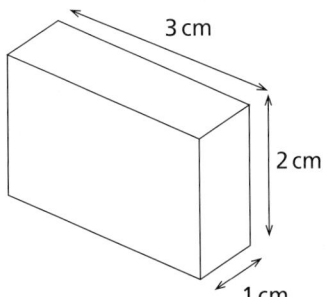

AQA(SEG) 1998

T2 Here is a plan view of a solid made from four cubes.

Here is a view of the solid from direction A.

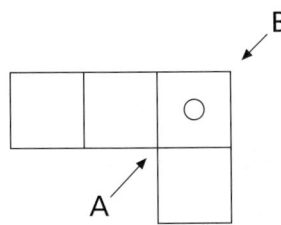

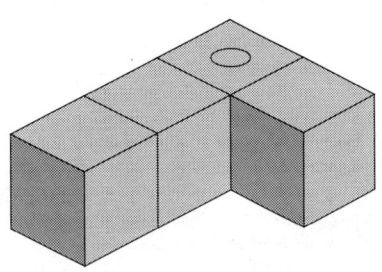

On sheet P125, complete the drawing to show the view from direction B.
Use a pencil so that you can rub out any mistakes.

OCR(MEG)

T3 Sheet P126 shows two shapes.
Draw in one plane of symmetry for each of these shapes.

Edexcel

T4 This is a sketch of a house.

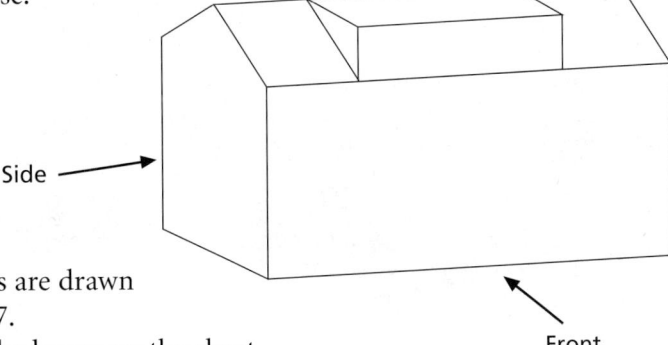

The front and side views are drawn accurately on sheet P127.
Draw the plan view of the house on the sheet.

OCR

6 3D puzzles • 55

7 Solving equations

You should know
- that an expression such as $x + x + x$ is equivalent to $3 \times x$ or $3x$.
- how to simplify an expression such as $2x + 5 + x - 4$

You will learn how to
- solve equations such as $3x - 1 = x + 5$ by balancing
- form and solve equations to solve problems

A Balancing puzzles

A1 The scales balance in these pictures.
Find the weight of each object.

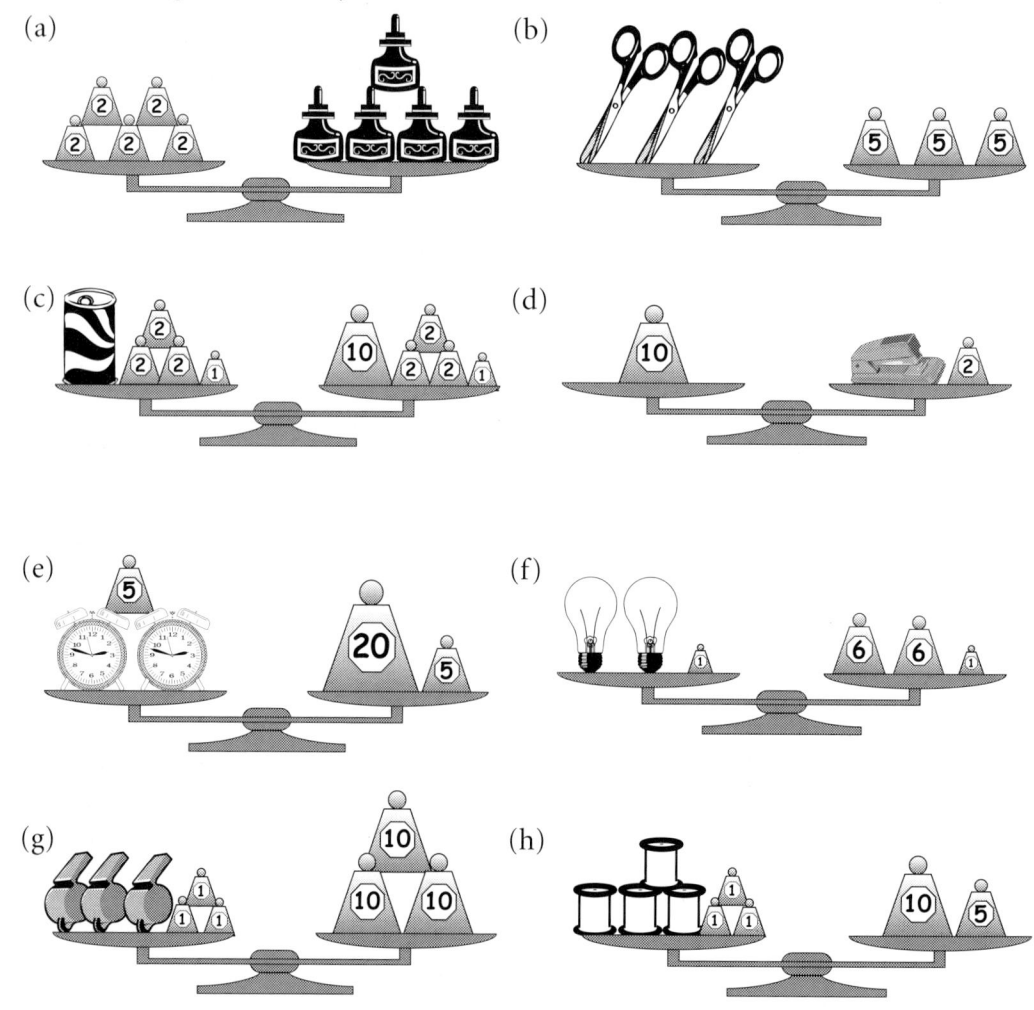

A2 The scales balance in these pictures.
Find the weight of each object.

(a)

(b)

(c)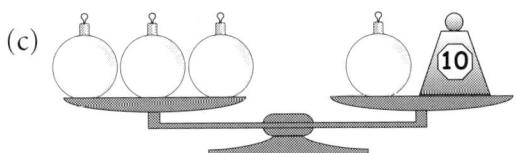

(d)

(e)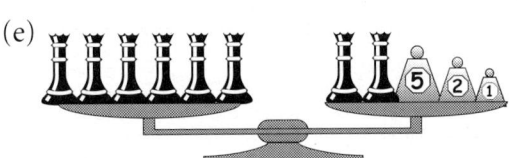

(f)

(g)

(h)

(i)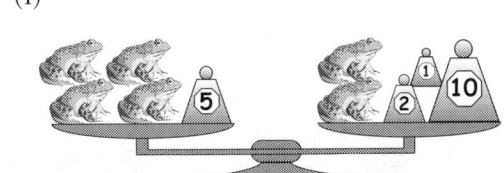

(j)

B Balancing and equations

We can write a balance puzzle as an equation using shorthand.

This puzzle can be written as $x + x + x = x + 10$
or $3x = x + 10$

The solution can be written $x = 5$

x stands for the weight of a bauble.

This is shorthand for 'The weight of a bauble is 5.'

B1 Here is a set of equations.

(a) $5x + 3 = 13$ (b) $2x + 9 = 15$ (c) $x + 16 = 3x$

(d) $6x = 4x + 12$ (e) $3x + 2 = x + 10$ (f) $5x + 1 = 2x + 13$

For each equation
- write down the balance puzzle that matches it
- solve the puzzle and write down the solution in the form '$x = ...$'

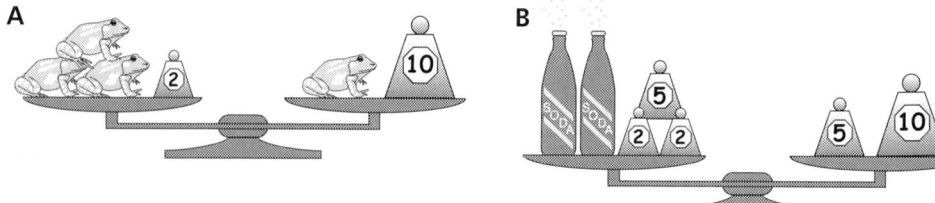

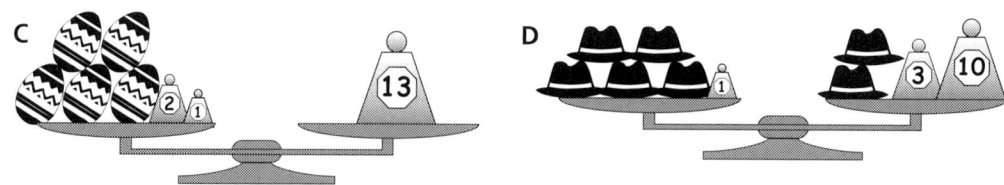

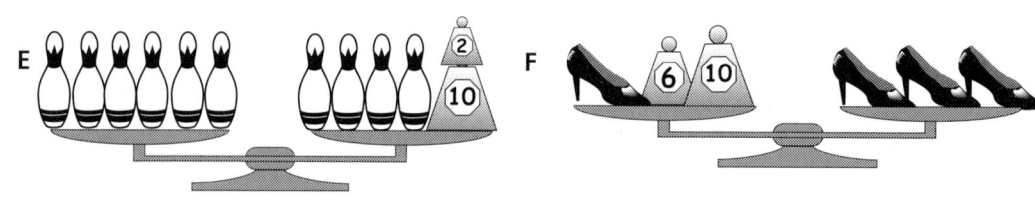

C Solving equations

We can solve equations by thinking of them as balance puzzles.

Example

Use balancing to solve the equation $7x + 3 = 2x + 23$.

First we can take $2x$ away from each side.

Now we can take 3 away from each side.

Last we can divide both sides by 5.

Now we can check the solution.

$7x + 3 = 2x + 23$
$-2x \qquad -2x$
$5x + 3 = 23$
$-3 \qquad -3$
$5x = 20$
$\div 5 \qquad \div 5$
$x = 4$

Check
left side: $(7 \times 4) + 3 = 31$
right side: $(2 \times 4) + 23 = 31$
so both sides balance.

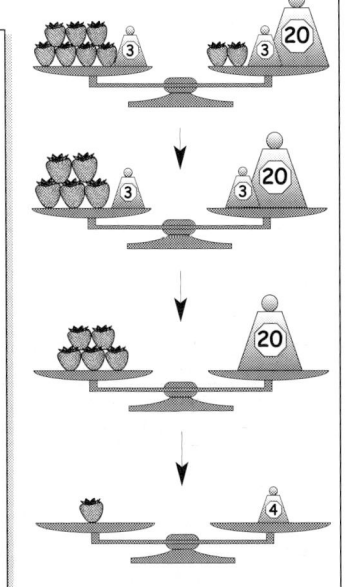

C1 Use balancing to solve these equations.
(Show your working clearly and check each answer.)
(a) $3x + 5 = 14$ (b) $2x + 3 = 17$ (c) $4x + 1 = 17$
(d) $5x + 6 = 31$ (e) $7x + 2 = 23$ (f) $6x + 5 = 35$

C2 Use balancing to solve these equations.
(a) $2x = x + 7$ (b) $5x = 3x + 8$ (c) $4x = 3x + 9$
(d) $9x = 4x + 15$ (e) $2x + 10 = 3x$ (f) $4x + 9 = 7x$

C3 Use balancing to solve these equations.
(a) $2x + 3 = x + 11$ (b) $6x + 1 = 5x + 6$ (c) $3x + 5 = x + 11$
(d) $9x + 2 = x + 18$ (e) $4x + 3 = 2x + 7$ (f) $7x + 4 = 4x + 16$
(g) $7x + 3 = 2x + 23$ (h) $3x + 9 = 5x + 7$ (i) $2x + 9 = 6x + 1$

C4 (a) Write down an equation for this puzzle. Use x to stand for the weight of a tin.

(b) Solve the equation to find the weight of a tin.

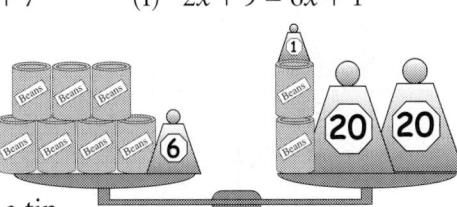

D Strips

What does *x* stand for in each diagram?

D1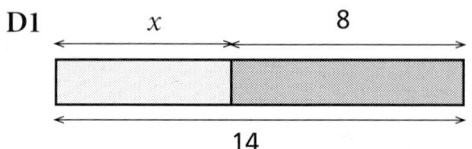

D2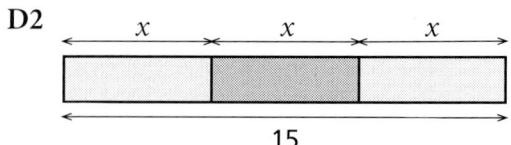

D3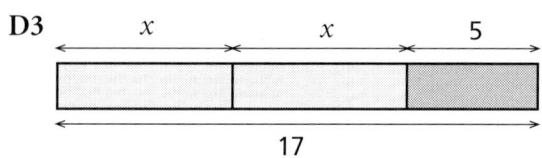

D4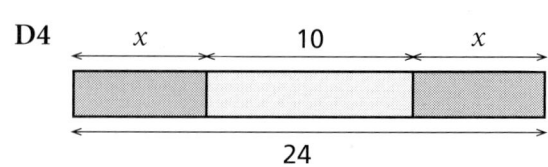

D5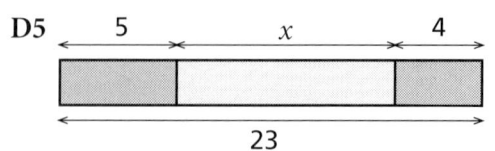

D6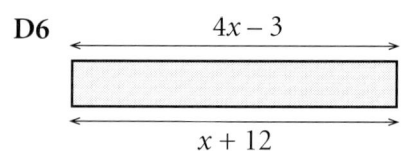

D7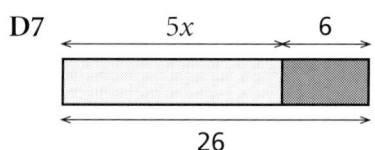

D8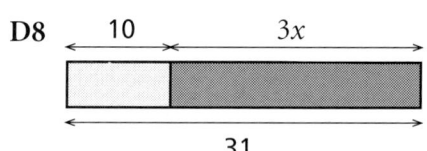

D9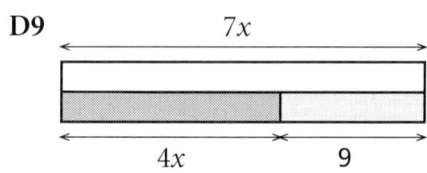

D10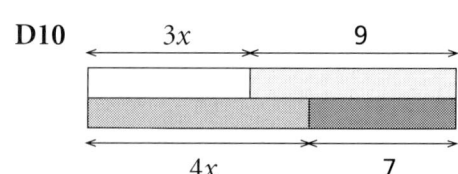

D11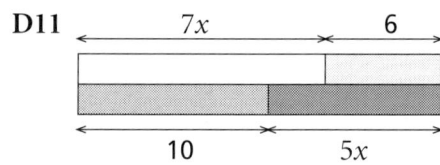

D12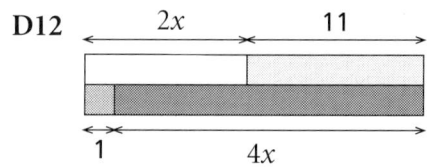

D13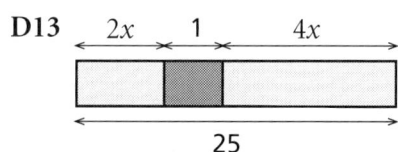

D14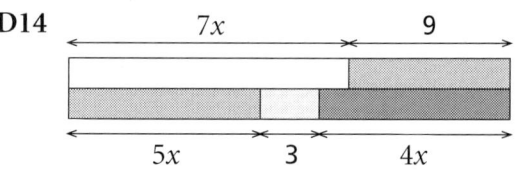

E Undoing subtractions

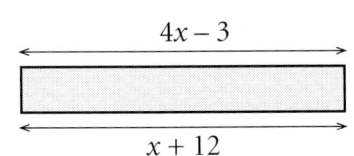

To find the value of x for this strip, we can solve the equation

$4x - 3 = x + 12$.

First we can add 3 to each side.

Now we can take x off each side.

Lastly we can divide both sides by 3.

Now we can check the solution.

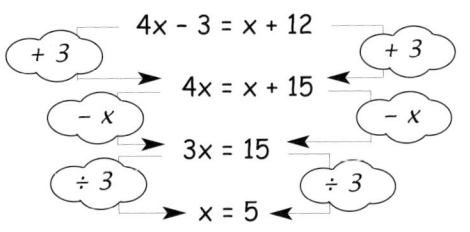

E1 Solve these equations.
(a) $x - 4 = 5$
(b) $x - 12 = 3$
(c) $2x - 1 = 11$
(d) $3x - 7 = 5$
(e) $4x - 1 = 11$
(f) $5x - 12 = 8$
(g) $2x - 3 = 15$
(h) $3x - 2 = 19$
(i) $6x - 5 = 1$

E2 Solve these equations.
(a) $5x - 1 = 4x + 3$
(b) $2x - 3 = x + 5$
(c) $5x - 2 = 3x + 4$
(d) $x + 1 = 2x - 1$
(e) $2x + 1 = 3x - 2$
(f) $4x - 9 = x + 6$
(g) $3x + 8 = 5x - 12$
(h) $x + 15 = 6x - 15$
(i) $5x - 5 = 2x + 16$

E3 Work out the value of x for each strip.
(a)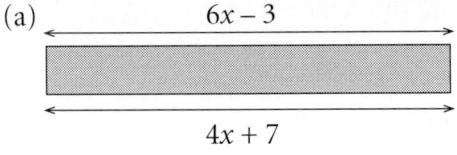
(b)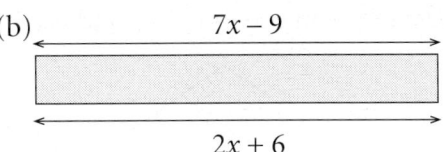

*** E4** Solve these equations.
(a) $2x = 5x - 9$
(b) $6x - 12 = 4x$
(c) $x = 3x - 10$
(d) $4x - 6 = 3x - 1$
(e) $5x - 7 = 3x - 1$
(f) $4x - 25 = x - 1$

F Problem solving

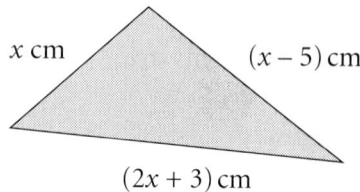

The perimeter of this triangle is 30 cm.
- Find the value of x and sketch the triangle.

F1 (a) Find an expression, in terms of x, for the perimeter of this rectangle. Give your answer in its simplest form.

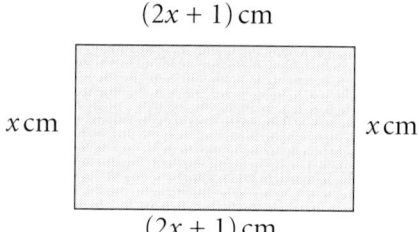

The perimeter of the rectangle is 44 cm.

(b) Write down an equation and solve it to find the value of x.

F2 The length of the sides of a triangle are $(x + 1)$ cm, $(x + 3)$ cm and $(x - 2)$ cm, as shown.

(a) Write an expression, in terms of x, for the perimeter of the triangle. Give your answer in its simplest form.

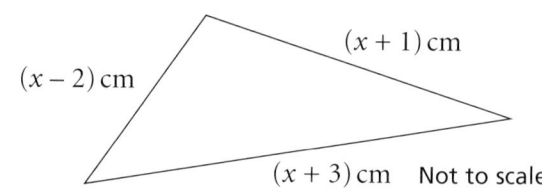

Not to scale

The perimeter is 23 cm.

(b) Write down an equation in x and use it to find the value of x. *AQA(SEG) 2000 Specimen*

F3 (a) Write an expression for the sum of the angles marked in this triangle. Give your answer in its simplest form.

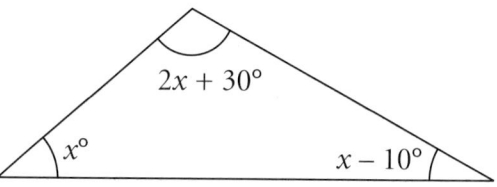

The angles of a triangle add up to 180°.

(b) Write down an equation in x and use it to find the value of x.

F4

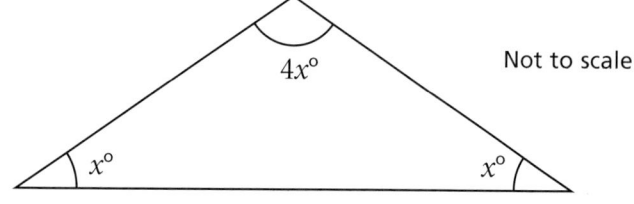

Not to scale

(a) Write down an equation involving x.

(b) Solve your equation to find the value of x. *OCR*

62 • 7 Solving equations

G Not always wholly positive

G1 Solve these equations and write each answer as a decimal.
(a) $2x = 7$
(b) $5n + 3 = 4$
(c) $2x - 3 = 2$
(d) $6p + 1 = 2p + 7$
(e) $5x + 2 = 3x + 7$
(f) $2y + 4 = 7y - 3$

G2 Solve these equations. Each solution is a negative number.
(a) $x + 5 = 4$
(b) $n + 8 = 5$
(c) $2x + 3 = {}^-1$
(d) $y + 8 = 2y + 10$
(e) $3x + 10 = x + 4$
(f) $5a + 5 = 2a - 16$

G3 Solve these equations.
(a) $5p + 12 = {}^-3$
(b) $4x - 1 = 2x + 5$
(c) $2n + 5 = n + 9$
(d) $n + 5 = 2n + 9$
(e) $5y + 20 = 2y + 8$
(f) $2x - 1 = 4x + 5$

Test yourself with these questions

T1 Solve
(a) $x + 5 = 12$
(b) $5x = 3x + 8$
OCR

T2 Solve
(a) $x - 5 = 13$
(b) $2y + 3 = 17$
(c) $2n + 1 = 3n - 2$
AQA(SEG) 1998 Specimen

T3 Solve these equations
(a) $3x - 5 = 7$
(b) $3x + 2 = 5x - 10$
OCR

T4 Solve
(a) $5x - 3 = 7$
(b) $5x + 5 = 7 + x$
AQA(NEAB) 1998

T5 Solve
(a) $2x = 10$
(b) $6y + 1 = 25$
(c) $8p - 3 = 3p + 13$
Edexcel

T6 The angles of a triangle are $(2x - 3)°$, $(x + 4)°$ and $(x + 19)°$.

(a) Write an expression, in terms of x, for the sum of the angles. Give your answer in its simplest form.

The sum of the angles is 180°.

(b) (i) Write down an equation in x.
(ii) Solve your equation to find the size of the **smallest** angle in the triangle.
AQA(SEG) 1998

T7 Solve
(a) $3x + 7 = 1$
(b) $2x + 3 = 7x + 8$

8 Finding and using formulas

You will revise
- forming and simplifying expressions with letters in them

The work will help you learn about
- forming more complicated expressions with powers in them
- forming an expression or formula from number machines and puzzles

A Review: substitution

Be expressive! A game for 2 players.

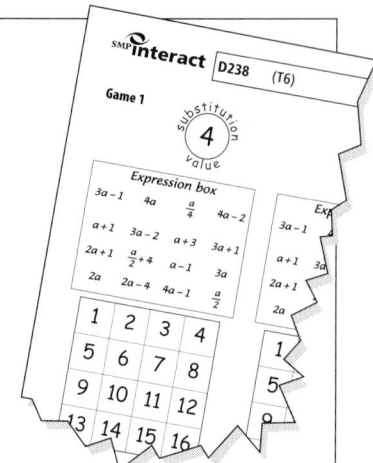

You need sheet P128

Players take turns

Player 1

Pick any expression from the expression box.
Put the substitution value into the expression, and work out the result.
Put a cross on the square with that result in it.
Then cross out the expression you used.

Player 2

Do the same, but put a circle on the square with the result in.

Winner

The first player with three in a line.

A1 For each pair of expressions, say which is larger when $n = 6$.
 (a) $3n$ and $n + 8$ (b) $\frac{1}{2}n$ and $n - 4$ (c) $2n$ and $n + 5$

A2 Evaluate each of these expressions when $x = 8$.
 (a) $3x + 1$ (b) $4x - 5$ (c) $\frac{1}{2}x + 3$ (d) $2x - 16$
 (e) $\frac{x}{2} - 1$ (f) $2x + 14$ (g) $\frac{x+4}{2}$ (h) $\frac{x-4}{4}$

A3 In each part, work out which expression is biggest when $a = 5$.
 (a) $3a - 12$ $\frac{a+9}{2}$ $5a - 20$ $2a + 1$
 (b) $\frac{a}{5} + 10$ $4a - 10$ $2a + 2$ $\frac{a+13}{2}$

A4 For each part of question A3, work out which expression is biggest when $a = 10$.

A5 Copy and complete this working to evaluate $3(a + 2)$ when $a = 5$.

```
3(a + 2)  when a = 5
= 3 × (   )
= 3 × 
=
```

A6 Work out each of these.
(a) $2(a + 3)$ when $a = 5$
(b) $3(b - 2)$ when $b = 10$
(c) $4(c + 1)$ when $c = 9$
(d) $5(1 + d)$ when $d = 2$

A7 When $x = 5$, which is bigger: $2(x + 3)$ or $2x + 3$?

B Taking off

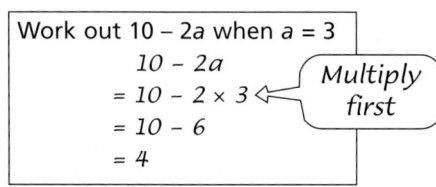

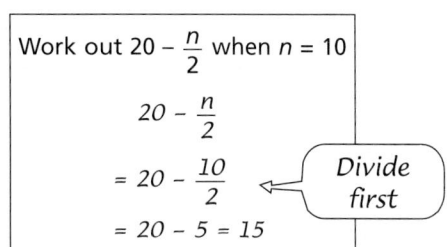

B1 (a) Copy and complete this working to evaluate $10 - 3a$ when $a = 2$.

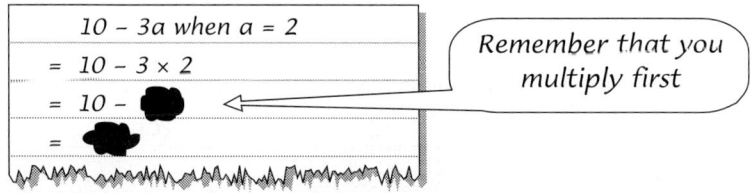

(b) Evaluate each of these expressions when $n = 6$.
(i) $10 + 4n$ (ii) $20 - 3n$ (iii) $100 - 10n$ (iv) $20 + 5n$

B2 (a) When $x = 10$, evaluate $40 - \frac{x}{2}$. (Remember to work out the value of $\frac{x}{2}$ first.)

(b) Evaluate each of these expressions when $n = 10$.
(i) $8 + \frac{n}{2}$ (ii) $20 - \frac{n}{2}$ (iii) $100 - \frac{n}{2}$ (iv) $20 + \frac{n}{2}$

B3 In this triangle, angle ACB is $2k + 20°$, and ABC is $3k - 10°$.
(a) If $k = 5$
  (i) how big is angle ACB in degrees?
  (ii) how big is angle ABC?
  (iii) work out angle CAB.
(b) (i) What size is each angle when $k = 30$?
  (ii) What special name does the triangle have when $k = 30$?

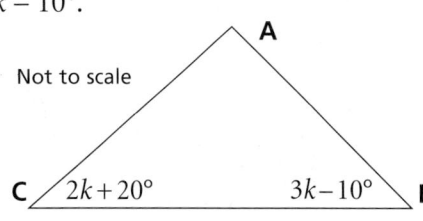

C Areas

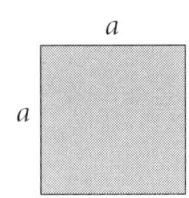

Area = a × a
     = a^2

When a = 5,
Area = $a^2 = 5^2$
     = 5 × 5 = 25

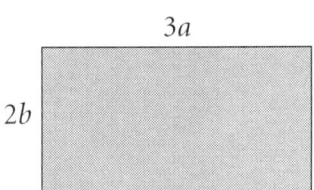

Area = 3a × 2b
     = 3 × a × 2 × b
     = 3 × 2 × a × b
     = 6ab

When a = 3 and b = 2,
Area = 6ab
     = 6 × 3 × 2 = 36

C1 (a) Write down and simplify an expression for the area of this rectangle.

(b) What are the lengths of the sides when p = 2 and q = 3?

(c) Substitute p = 2 and q = 3 into your expression for the area. Use your answer to part (b) to check your result is correct.

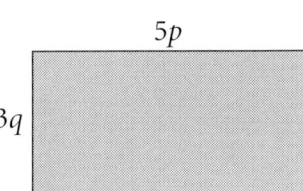

C2 Write down and simplify expressions for the areas of these shapes.

(a) 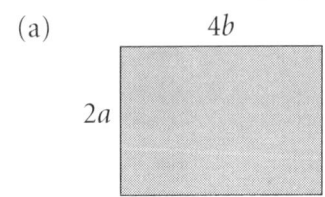   (b) 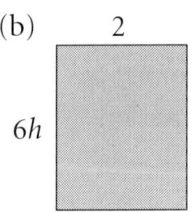   (c)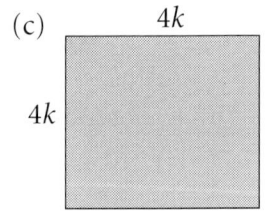

C3 Simplify each of these expressions.

(a) 3a × 5b   (b) 4 × 5x   (c) 3y × 4y   (d) k × 5l   (e) 5e × 4e
(f) 2n × 2n   (g) 4m × 5   (h) 6j × 5k   (i) 2r × 3s   (j) 5a × b

C4 Work out an expression for the missing side in each of these shapes.

(a) 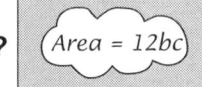   (b) 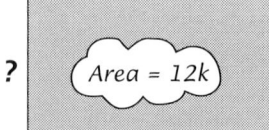   (c)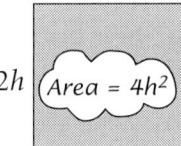

66 • 8 Finding and using formulas

D More letters

$a = 2, b = 3, c = 6$

$10 - ab$	$5ab$	$4(a+b)$	$2b^2$	$\dfrac{c}{a}$
$= 10 - a \times b$	$= 5 \times a \times b$	$= 4 \times (2+3)$	$= 2 \times b \times b$	
$= 10 - 2 \times 3$	$= 5 \times 2 \times 3$	$= 4 \times 5$	$= 2 \times 3 \times 3$	$= \dfrac{6}{2}$
$= 10 - 6 = 4$	$= 30$	$= 20$	$= 18$	$= 3$

D1 Work out these when $p = 2$ and $q = 3$.
(a) pq (b) $5 + pq$ (c) $pq - 4$ (d) $5pq$ (e) $5pq + 10$

D2 Work these out when $u = 4$, $v = 8$ and $w = 24$.
(a) $\dfrac{v}{u}$ (b) $10 + \dfrac{v}{u}$ (c) $\dfrac{w}{u} - 1$ (d) $\dfrac{w}{u} + 10$ (e) $\dfrac{w}{u} + v$

D3 If $a = 2$, $b = 6$ and $c = 5$, work out
(a) $3(a+b)$ (b) $3a + 4b$ (c) $10(c-a)$ (d) $6(b-c)$ (e) $4c - 3b$

D4 If $r = 4$, $s = 5$ and $t = 2$, work out
(a) $3t^2$ (b) $2s^2$ (c) r^2 (d) $r^2 - 6$ (e) $\dfrac{r^2}{2}$

D5

T	F	E	R	L	W	N	B	G	U	H	A
24	13	8	12	9	36	1	18	2	10	3	6

Work out each of the expressions below when $a = 2$, $b = 3$ and $c = 6$.
Then find the letter in the box above.
Unjumble the letters in each part to make a word.

(a) ab $\dfrac{c}{a}$ $3(a+c)$ c^2

(b) $2(a+b)$ $a^2 + 9$ $2ab - 11$

(c) bc $\dfrac{c}{b}$ b^2 $2b+c$ ba $b + \dfrac{c}{a}$ $2a^2$

D6 $P = 2l + 2w$.
$l = 12$ and $w = 8$. Work out the value of P. *Edexcel*

D7 When $u = 5$ and $v = 4$, work out
(a) $2v^2$ (b) $\dfrac{v^2}{2}$ (c) u^2 (d) $u^2 + v^2$ (e) $u^2 - v^2$

D8 a^3 means $a \times a \times a$. Work out
(a) a^3 when $a = 2$ (b) x^3 when $x = 3$ (c) n^3 when $n = 1$

D9 With a partner, play the games on sheet P129.

E Arrow diagrams

Suppose that 8 is put into this arrow diagram…

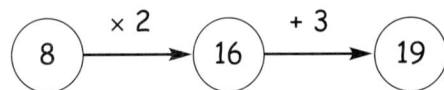

…then 19 is the result.

Let n stand for the number that is put in…

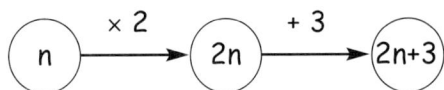

…then the result is $2n + 3$.
If r stands for the result, we can write a formula for r in terms of n
$$r = 2n + 3$$

E1 For each of these arrow diagrams
- work out the result when 8 is put in
- if r stands for the result when n is put in, write a formula for r in terms of n.

(a) 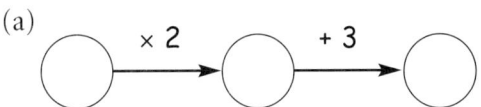   (b)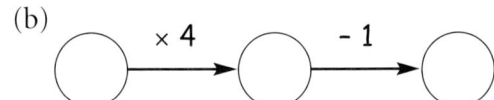

(c) 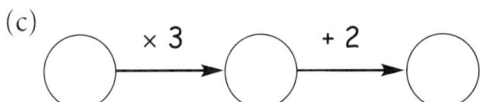   (d)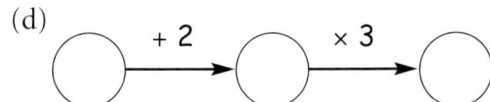

E2 Match these three arrow diagrams with the formulas on the right.
n stands for the number that is input; r stands for the result.

A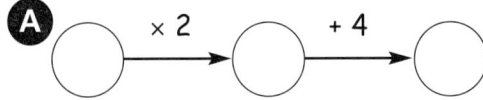

J $r = \dfrac{n}{2} + 4$

B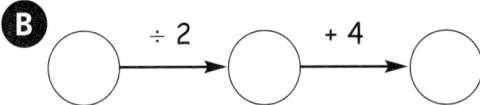

K $r = 2n + 4$

C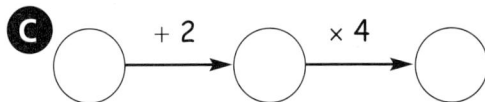

L $r = 4(n + 2)$

E3 Suppose x is put into this arrow diagram.
Let y stand for the number that comes out.
Write a formula for x in terms of y.

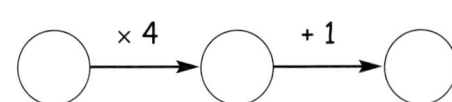

F Using and making formulas

F1 Some frameworks are made from long and short struts.
The length of a long strut is L cm.
The length of a short strut is S cm.

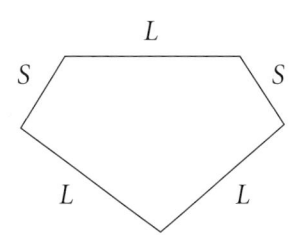

(a) Write down a formula for the perimeter,
R cm, of this framework.
Write the formula as simply as possible.
Start it with $R = \ldots$

(b) The formula for the perimeter, P cm, of a different framework is $P = 6L + 3S$.
If $L = 5$ and $S = 2$, work out the perimeter of this framework. OCR

F2 (a) Write down and simplify an expression
for the perimeter of this rectangle.

(b) Write an expression for the area of the rectangle.
Write the expression as simply as possible.

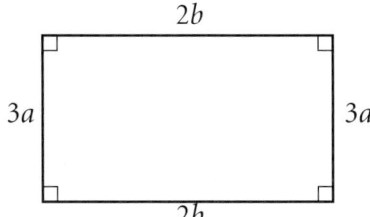

F3 Chris is a programmer. His wages each month, £W,
are calculated using a formula.

$$W = 7h - 5n$$

h is the number of hours he works.
n is the number of mistakes he makes.

(a) Work out W when $h = 100$ and $n = 10$.

(b) In March, Chris works for 100 hours and
makes 20 mistakes. Work out W.

(c) In April he works for 200 hours and makes 40 mistakes.
What will his wages be?

(d) In May he works for 50 hours but makes 70 mistakes!
What will his wages be?

F4 The Beeches hotel caters for wedding parties.
The hotel uses this formula to work out the cost. $C = 10n + 50$.
C is the cost in pounds, n is the number of people in the party.

(a) What will it cost for a party of 30 people?

(b) Another hotel, The Oaks, uses this formula.
Write this as a formula connecting C and n.

C is the cost in pounds,
n is the number of people in the party.

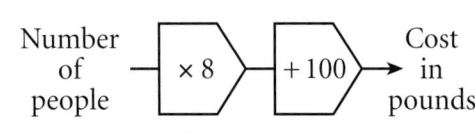

OCR

F5 (a) Ken starts with 3.
What is his answer?

(b) Lubna starts with x.
What is her answer?

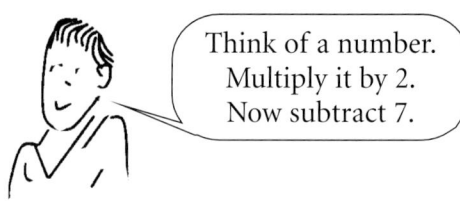

AQA 2003 Specimen

F6 Each year the High School has a disco for year 7.
A teacher works out how many cans of drink to buy, using this rule.

> 2 cans for each ticket sold, plus 20 spare cans.

(a) This year, 160 tickets have been sold. How many cans will he buy?

(b) Using N for the number of cans, and T for the number of tickets, write down the teacher's formula for N in terms of T.

AQA 2003 Specimen

F7 Mila is having a party. She uses this rule to work out how many litre bottles of drink to buy.

> number of bottles = number of people ÷ 2, plus another 10 bottles.

(a) How many bottles will she buy if she expects 40 people?

(b) How many bottles will she buy if she expects 100 people.

(c) Write the rule as a formula.
Use N to stand for the number of bottles, and p to stand for the number of people.

Test yourself with these questions

T1 Evaluate each of these expressions when $x = 8$.
(a) $5x$
(b) $x + 12$
(c) $\dfrac{x}{4}$
(d) $x - 3$
(e) $\frac{1}{2}x$

T2 Evaluate each of theses when $n = 10$.
(a) $2n - 4$
(b) $3n + 12$
(c) $\dfrac{n}{2} + 3$
(d) $\dfrac{n+2}{3}$
(e) $3 + 2n$

T3 Work out each of these.
(a) $3(a + 2)$ when $a = 6$
(b) $2(b - 3)$ when $b = 8$
(c) $4(c - 1)$ when $c = 7$
(d) $4(1 + d)$ when $d = 9$
(e) $5 + 3e$ when $e = 2$
(f) $12 - 2f$ when $f = 5$
(g) $12 - 3g$ when $g = 4$
(h) $4 + \dfrac{h}{2}$ when $h = 6$

T4 The cost of tipping waste can be worked out using this formula.

> Cost in £ = 15 × Weight in tonnes + Handling charge

At my local tip, the handling charge is £30.
How much will it cost to tip 5 tonnes of waste?

T5 Look at these shapes.

Write as simply as possible an expression for

(a) the perimeter of the triangle,

(b) the perimeter of the rectangle,

(c) the area of the rectangle.

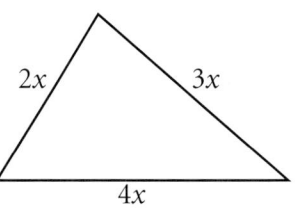
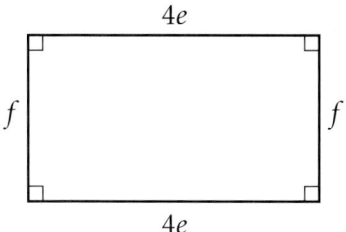

OCR

T6 Work out these when $e = 2$, $f = 5$ and $g = 6$.

(a) $ef + 2$ (b) $ef - 4$ (c) $5eg + 10$ (d) $3(f + g)$ (e) $10(g - f)$

(f) $2e + 3f$ (g) f^2 (h) $2f^2$ (i) $g^2 - 20$ (j) $g^2 - f^2$

T7 Evaluate when $p = 8$, $q = 2$ and $r = 4$

(a) $\frac{p}{q} - 3$ (b) q^3 (c) $\frac{r^2}{8}$ (d) $10 - \frac{r}{q}$ (e) $q + \frac{p}{r}$

T8 If $a = 3$, $b = 4$ and $c = \frac{1}{2}$, work out the value of

(a) $2a + 3b$ (b) $a - b + 3c$

AQA 2003 Specimen

T9 Kareem drives a taxi. He uses a formula to work out his charge in pounds.

> Divide the number of miles by 2. And then add 10.

Work out Kareem's charge for a journey of 48 miles.

OCR

T10 A builder calculates the cost of his work, in pounds, using this formula.

> Multiply the number of hours worked by 8, then add 12.

(a) What is the cost of his work for a job which takes 6 hours?

(b) What is the cost of his work for a job which takes $\frac{1}{2}$ hour?

(c) Write a formula connecting C and n
where C is the cost in pounds
            n is the number of hours worked.

OCR

T11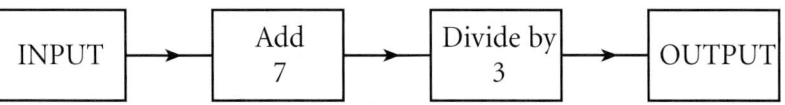

(a) When the input is 17, what is the output?

(b) Let the input number be x. Write down the output in terms of x.

WJEC

Review 1

1. For the rule $y = 2x - 4$
   (a) What is y when $x = 3$?
   (b) Copy and complete this table.

x	0	1	2	3	4	5
y	-4					

   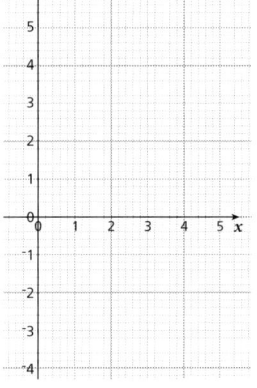

   (c) On axes like the ones on the right, plot the points from your table. Join the points with a line.
   (d) From the graph, what is y when x is 3.5?
   (e) What is the value of x when y is -1?

2. On squared paper, draw axes with both x and y going from -3 to 3.
   On your axes, draw and label the lines $y = -2$ and $x = 3$.

3. Round to one significant figure
   (a) 375   (b) 409   (c) 0.468   (d) 0.076   (e) 1.005

4. Work out a rough estimate for the total weight of each of these. Show your working.
   (a) 39 books that weigh 2.1 kg each
   (b) 5.9 metres of lead strip that weighs 3.06 kg per metre
   (c) 79 cars that weigh 1.075 tonnes each

5. Calculate each of the lettered angles.

   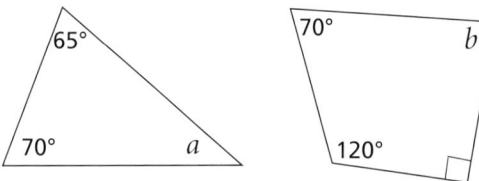
   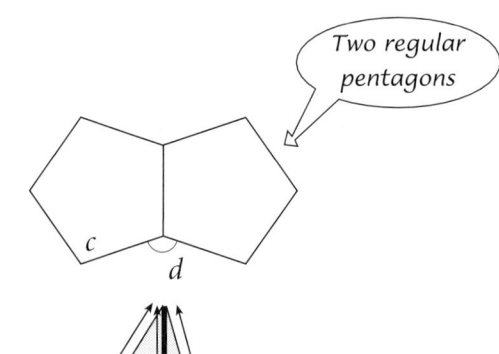

   Two regular pentagons

6. This yacht has two sails, A and B.
   Work out the area of each sail.
   (You may not need to use all the measurements that are given.)

   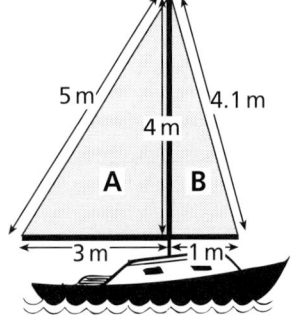

7 Consecutive numbers are whole numbers that are next to each other, like 11 and 12.
Find two consecutive numbers that multiply together to give 3192.

8 A cube has a volume of 80 cm³.
Use a table like this one to find the length
of an edge correct to 1 decimal place.

Length of an edge	Volume	Result too small	too large
6	216		✓

9 This solid is made from 5 centimetre cubes.

(a) Does the solid have any planes of symmetry?
If so, how many?

(b) On squared paper, draw a plan view, a front
view and a side view of the solid.

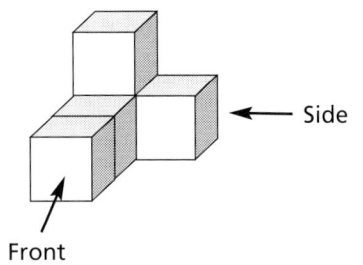

10 Solve these equations.

(a) $x + 3 = 15$ (b) $4x + 1 = 13$ (c) $x - 3 = 11$

(d) $4x = 2x + 10$ (e) $x + 5 = 2x + 1$ (f) $5x + 4 = 3x + 10$

11 Solve

(a) $2x - 3 = 11$ (b) $4x - 7 = x + 5$ (c) $2x + 11 = 5x - 4$

12 (a) Write down and simplify an expression
for the sum of the angles of this triangle.

(b) The angles of a triangle add up to 180°.
Use this fact and your answer to part (a)
to write down an equation in x.

(c) Solve your equation, and use the solution to
work out the size of each angle of the triangle.

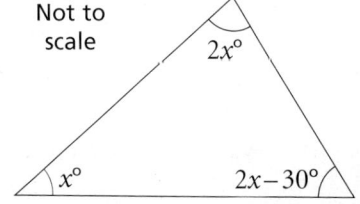

Not to scale

13 This shape is made from two different length rods.
One rod has length a cm, the other has length b cm.

Write down a formula for the perimeter, P cm, of the shape.
Write the formula as simply as possible.

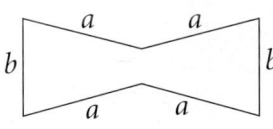

14 To cook a joint of beef, May allows 30 minutes per kilogram
plus another 20 minutes.

(a) How many minutes will May cook a 2 kg joint of beef for?

(b) How many minutes will she allow for a 3 kg joint?

(c) Write May's rule as a formula.
Use w to stand for the weight of the beef in kg
and t to stand for the time it takes to cook in minutes.

9 Ratio and proportion

You will learn how to
- find quantities by multiplying up from given proportions
- use the unitary method to find quantities from given proportions
- use unit costs to compare prices
- use ratios written in the form $a:b$
- share a total in a given ratio

A Recipes

Lemon Ice Cream
(makes 6 servings)

10 egg yolks
200 g caster sugar
50 ml lemon juice
400 ml double cream

Gooseberry Jam
(makes about 5 kg)

2 kg gooseberries
3 kg sugar
1 litre water

Fish Pie
(serves 4)

500 g haddock
400 ml milk
60 g butter
200 ml single cream
2 eggs
800 g potatoes

Spinach and panir curry
(serves 4)

30 ml oil
200 g panir (Indian cheese)
400 g spinach
3 tomatoes

Nice Nosh Catering Buffet menu
(Quantities needed for 50 people)

4 sliced loaves or 12 French sticks
1.8 kg of butter
10 tomatoes

Basic fillings for 12 sandwiches

400 g canned tuna fish
240 g coleslaw
10 hard boiled eggs

1 large sliced loaf can make 12 sandwiches.
100 g of butter can be spread on 12 sandwiches

Use the recipes opposite to answer these questions.

A1 How many eggs would you need to make fish pie for 8 people?

A2 How many of these items would you need
(a) tomatoes to make spinach and panir curry for 12 people,
(b) hard boiled eggs to make tuna sandwiches for 48 people,
(c) tomatoes for the Nice Nosh company to give a buffet for 150,
(d) eggs to make fish pie for 2 people,
(e) hard boiled eggs to make tuna sandwiches for 6 people,
(f) tomatoes to make spinach and panir curry for 2 people?

A3 How much would you need of these ingredients.
(a) butter to make a fish pie to serve 8 people,
(b) panir to make a spinach and panir curry for 12 people,
(c) coleslaw to make sandwiches for 48 people,
(d) sugar to make 20 kg of jam,
(e) butter for Nice Nosh to run a buffet for 25 people,
(f) spinach to make spinach and panir curry for two people?

A4 Copy and complete these recipes.

(a)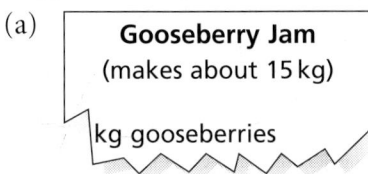
Gooseberry Jam
(makes about 15 kg)
... kg gooseberries

(b)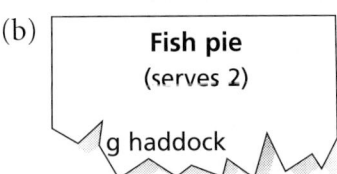
Fish pie
(serves 2)
... g haddock

A5 What number of people could you make fish pie for if you had plenty of all the other ingredients **but** only had
(a) 180 g of butter
(b) 10 eggs
(c) 1 kg of haddock?

A6 What number of people could you make spinach and panir curry for if you had plenty of all other ingredients but only had
(a) 90 ml of oil
(b) 18 tomatoes
(c) 1 kg of panir

A7 (a) How much butter would you need to make a fish pie for one person?
(b) Use this to find the amount of butter you would need to make a fish pie for
(i) 6 people.
(ii) 10 people.
(iii) 14 people.

A8 (a) How much tuna fish would you need to make 3 tuna sandwiches?
(b) How much tuna fish is needed to make
(i) 9 sandwiches
(ii) 15 sandwiches
(iii) 30 sandwiches

B Comparisons

In a supermarket packets of Lingos can be bought for 27p.

They can also be bought in a multipack with 6 packets costing £1.50.

27p Special price £1.50

- What would 6 packets of Lingos cost if they were bought separately?
- Is the multipack actually better value?

B1 In each of these examples
- find the cost of buying the items in the multipack separately
- decide whether the multipack actually gives you more for your money

(a) 48p a bottle   Multipack 8 bottles for £3.92

(b) 37p a box   Multipack 10 boxes for £3.50

(c) 95p a lolly   Multipack 12 lollies for £11.28

(d) £1.29 a tin   Multipack 8 tins for £10.56

B2 A large pack of Rougefort cheese weighs 500 g and costs £7.
A small pack weighs 100 g and costs £1.50

(a) How many small packs would you need to get the same weight as the large pack?

(b) What is the cost of buying this number of small packs?

(c) Do you save money by buying one of the larger packs?

B3 In each of these cases
- find out how many smaller units make up the larger one
- find out whether it saves money to buy the larger unit

(a) 200 ml of cream costs 85p
    600 ml costs £3.25

(b) 200 g of rice costs £1.20
    1 kg (1000 g) costs £6.25

(c) 125 g of tea costs £1.30
    500 g costs £4.99

(d) 100 g of sweets cost 80p
    250 g costs £1.95

B4 Packets of Henson's tea are sold in two sizes.

Which size is the better value for money?
You must show all your working.

Large 500g £2.45   Small 250g £1.25

AQA(SEG) 2000

C The unitary method

It is often useful to calculate how much is needed for one person or unit.

3 litres of paint cover 36 m². What area will 5 litres of the same paint cover?

This is called the **unitary method**.

C1 A garden centre uses 30 kg of compost to fill 6 tubs.
  (a) How much compost do they use to fill one tub?
  (b) How much compost do they need to fill 10 tubs?

C2 150 g of dried peas are needed to make pea soup for 5 people.
  (a) What weight of peas is needed to make enough soup for one person?
  (b) What weight of peas is needed to make soup for 20 people?

C3 A woman walks 6 miles in 2 hours.
  If she walks at the same pace how far can she walk in 5 hours?

C4 Amy and Tom make bird tables.
  To make 3 bird tables they need:
  15 m of wood
  3 wooden trays
  36 nails
  Write out a list of materials they would need to make 7 bird tables.

C5 An expedition company has lists of suggested meals.
  This is a list of food for one meal for 5 people.
  20 veggie sausages
  750 g rice
  5 litres of water
  Make a list of food they would need for 7 people.

C6 This is a recipe for pastry to make mince pies.
  (a) To make 30 mince pies what weight would you need of
    (i) flour   (ii) sugar   (iii) butter?
  (b) How many egg yolks would you need for 30 mince pies?

> **Pastry for Mince Pies**
> *(makes 20 pies)*
> 500 g wholewheat flour
> 180 g brown sugar
> 240 g of butter (chopped)
> 4 egg yolks
> 2-3 drops of vanilla essence

D Unit costs

D1 These are two offers for paving slabs at different garden centres.

Trimleys Special Offer — 6 paving slabs for only £48

Hedges & Co. This week only — 4 paving slabs for only £28

(a) On Trimleys' offer what is the cost for each paving slab?

(b) At Hedges & Co, what is the cost for each slab?

(c) Which offer gives you more slabs for your money?

D2 Here are two bags of potatoes at a supermarket.

(a) Work out the cost of 1 kg in the Family Pack.

(b) Work out the cost of 1 kg in the Value Pack.

(c) Which pack gives you more for your money?

Value Pack (3kg £1.47), Family Pack (5kg £2.60)

The cost of an item for 1 kilogram, 1 litre, 1 metre or whatever the item is measured in is called the **unit cost**.

Supermarkets often put a unit cost underneath price labels to help customers decide what is the best way to buy items.

POTATOES, King Ed. 10kg
Item Code: 4456
15.3p per kg

D3 Here are some more labels from different shops.
In each part use unit costs to decide which works out cheaper.

(a) 3 litres 135p | 2 litre 94p

(b) 5 kg £1.50 | 2 kg 62p

(c) 3 kg £2.16 | 5 kg £3.25

(d) 12 metres £6.60 | 14 metres £8.40

D4 A standard bottle of mineral water contains 1.5 litres and costs 96p.
A large bottle contains 2.5 litres and costs £1.50.

(a) What is the cost of one litre of water in the standard bottle?

(b) What is the cost of one litre in the large bottle?

(c) In which bottle does the water work out cheaper?

(d) Why might you prefer to buy the standard bottle?

D5 Ecowash washing liquid can be bought in four sizes:

Large 3 litre £4.32 | Standard 1 litre £1.49 | Economy 1.5 litre £2.13 | Travel 0.5 litre 78p

(a) Find the cost of 1 litre for each size.

(b) Write the sizes in order of price per litre, the cheapest first.

D6 Ambreen wants to find the unit cost of a 3 kg pack of bacon costing £2.42.
Her calculator gives the answer to 2.42 ÷ 3 as: `0.8066666`

(a) Round this number to 2 decimal places.

(b) What is the cost of 1 kg of bacon to the nearest penny?

D7 Find the unit cost of these to the nearest penny:

(a) 6 litres of oil costing £5.48   (b) 7 metres of cable costing £4.99

(c) 9 kg of potatoes costing £3.99   (d) icecream costing £3.95 for 1.5 litres

D8 A supermarket sells milk in four different sizes:

A: 1 litre for 93p   **B:** 0.5 l for 48p   **C:** 1.5 l for £1.37   **D:** 3 litres for £2.75

(a) Find the cost of 1 litre of each size.

(b) Which size works out cheapest at this supermarket?

When items are measured in millilitres or grams it is easier to use a larger unit than 1.

For the medium size ÷2 (200 g costs £1.32 / 100g costs 64p) ÷2

Medium — 200 g £1.32

Large — 500 g £3.36

For the large size ÷5 (500 g costs £3.36 / 100g costs 67p) ÷5

So the medium size works out cheaper.

D9 A wholefoods store sells ground almonds in four sizes:

S: 200 g for 90p   M: 300 g for £1.15   L: 500 g for £2.05   EL: 800 g for £3.50

Find the cost for 100 g in each size and decide which works out cheaper.

D10 Asco bath lotion is sold in two sizes.   The large size contains 400 ml and costs £1.
The family size contains 1000 ml and costs £2.60.

Which size is the best value for money?
You must show your working.

AQA(SEG) 2000

D11 Simla tea is sold in two sizes: Small: 100 g for 1.64   Large: 250 g for £4.25

(a) Find the cost of 50 g of tea for both sizes.

(b) Which of the sizes gives you more for your money?

D12 A shop sells mayonnaise in two sizes.

Which jar gives better value for money?
Show how you decide.

OCR

E Mixing

A drama club is mixing up orange squash for the interval of the school play.

The students mixed the drinks up in different ways.

These trays show how much squash each student mixed with water.

- Which students would have made drinks with the same strength?
- Which trays had the strongest concentration of orange squash? Which had the weakest?

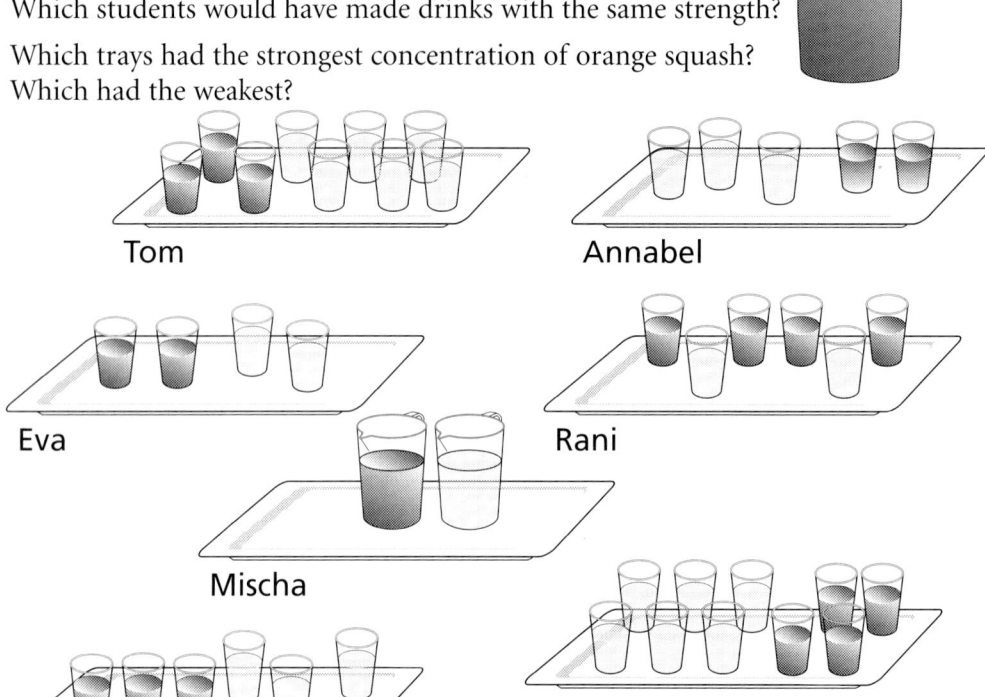

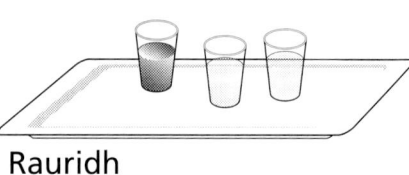

- Nina wants to make a drink the same strength as Rauridh. She has two mugs of squash. How much water does she need?

Ratio

If the squash is mixed so that every unit of squash is mixed with 4 of water, we say that

The ratio of squash to water is 1 to 4.

This is written as 1 : 4.

E1 Which of these mixtures show a ratio for squash to water of 1 : 4 ?
Where it is not, give the true ratio.

(a)

(b)

(c)

(d)

(e)

(f)

½ full

E2 Karl is making up some lemon squash.
He needs to use 6 parts of water for every part of juice.
Write TRUE or FALSE for each of these statements.

(a) The ratio of water to juice is 1:6. (b) The ratio of juice to water is 6:1.

(c) The ratio of water to juice is 6:1. (d) The ratio of juice to water is 1:6.

E3 To make porridge Moragh uses a ratio of oats to water of 1:3.

(a) How much water would she need to go with

(i) 4 cups of oats   (ii) 10 cups of oats   (iii) $1\frac{1}{2}$ cups of oats?

(b) How much oats would she need to go with

(i) 6 cups of water   (ii) 15 cups of water   (iii) 600 ml of water?

E4 To make shortcrust pastry you use flour and margarine in the ratio 2:1.

(a) How much margarine would you need to go with 500 g of flour?

(b) If you only had 150 g of margarine, how much flour would you need to use?

(c) If you used 300 g of flour

(i) How much margarine do you need?

(ii) What will be the weight of the flour and margarine mixed together?

E5 Concrete is made by mixing ballast and cement.
Different mixtures are used for different types of job.

Job	Cement	Ballast	Ratio cement to ballast
General	1 part	5 parts	1 : 5
Foundations	1 part		1 : 6
Paving	1 part	4 parts	

(a) Copy and complete the table above.

(b) What job would these mixtures be used for:
   (i) 2 buckets of cement and 10 of ballast
   (ii) 3 bags of cement and 12 bags of ballast?

(c) How much ballast would you need with
   (i) 3 buckets of cement to make concrete for foundations
   (ii) 10 wheelbarrows of cement to make concrete for general use?

(d) How much cement would you need with
   (i) 12 shovels of ballast to make concrete for foundations
   (ii) 20 bags of ballast to make concrete for general use?

(e) Charlie is making cement for paving and uses 12 pots of cement.
   (i) How much ballast does she need?
   (ii) How many pots of the mixture will she have in total?

E6 In a three legged race the ratio of 'legs' to people is 3 : 2.
(a) How many people are there if there are 9 'legs'?
(b) How many 'legs' are there if there are 18 people?
(c) What is the ratio of heads to 'legs'?
(d) What is the ratio of arms to 'legs'?

*__E7__ To make wholemeal flaky pastry you use flour and fat in the ratio 4 : 3.
(a) How much fat would you use with 400 g of flour?
(b) How much flour would you use with 600 g of fat?
(c) How much fat would you use with 200 g of flour?
(d) How much flour would you use with 60 g of fat?
(e) How much fat would you use with 1 kg of flour?
(f) How much flour would you use with 1 kg of fat?

F Simplest form

Which pairs of mixtures in this diagram have the same ratio?

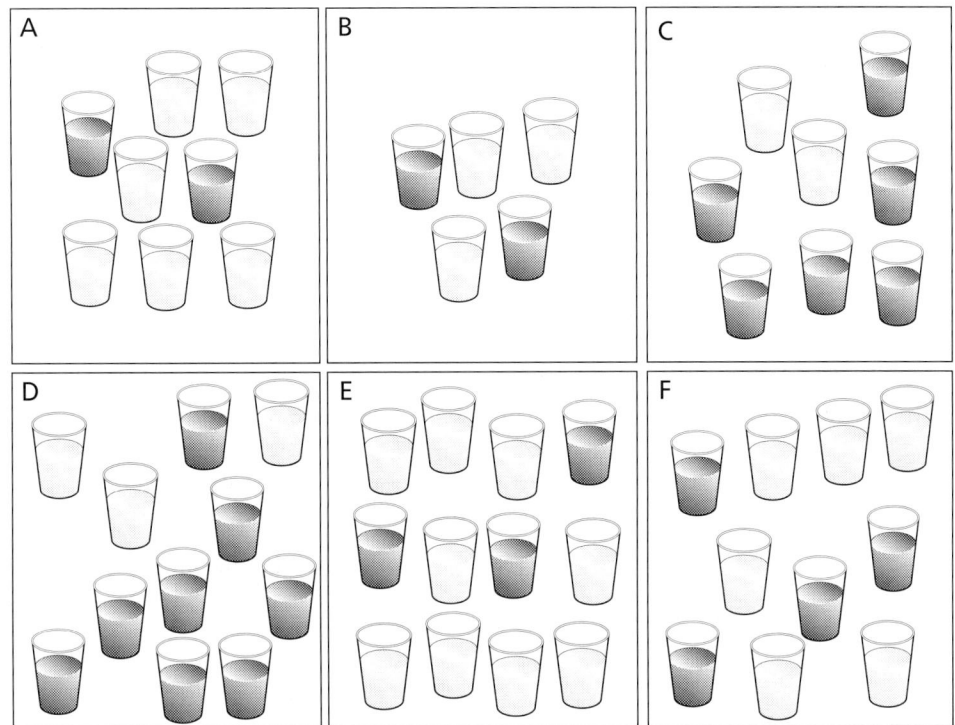

It is often useful to write a ratio in its **simplest form**.

Ratios can be reduced to simplest form in the same way as fractions by dividing both sides by common factors.

$$\begin{array}{c} 30:75 \\ \div 5 \downarrow \quad \quad \downarrow \div 5 \\ 6:15 \\ \div 3 \downarrow \quad \quad \downarrow \div 3 \\ 2:5 \end{array}$$

F1 Write these ratios in their simplest form.

(a) 8 : 24   (b) 21 : 15   (c) 18 : 36   (d) 24 : 60

(e) 144 : 60   (f) 28 : 84   (g) 120 : 300   (h) 500 : 2400

F2 A recipe says that you should use 150 g of fat and 250 g of flour.
Write the ratio of fat to flour in its simplest form.

F3 Write these as ratios in their simplest form

(a) A school has 240 boys and 300 girls.

(b) A school has 60 teachers and 900 pupils.

(c) A football match had 2700 United supporters and 3600 City supporters.

(d) A cat charity has 200 female members and 25 males.

G Sharing in a ratio

Fair shares

Martin and David have been earning money by washing windows.

They have earned £40 altogether.

They are discussing, with Mum's and Dad's help, how to share the money.

How much would they get with each suggestion?

Martin is 15, David is 9.

I think it should be in the ratio of ages. I'm 15 and you're only 9.

Well I did 14 windows, you only did 6.

You should share it in the ratio 2:3 with Martin getting the most.

I don't see why you can't just share it equally.

To share something in a given ratio you first have to find how many 'shares' there are.

To share £20 in the ratio 2 : 3 we say   Altogether there are 2 + 3 = 5 shares.
So 1 share is worth £20 ÷ 5 = £4.
The first person gets 2 × £4 = £8
The second person gets 3 × £4 = £12

Check: £8 + £12 = £20 so all the money is shared!

G1 What does each person get in these cases?

(a) £36 is shared in the ratio 5 : 4

(b) 64 marbles are shared in the ratio 3 : 5

(c) £120 is shared in the ratio 5 : 1

(d) 15 deliveries are shared in the ratio 2 : 3

G2 A farmer has 24 sheep.
He decides to give them to his sons in the ratio of their ages.
Geraint is 5, Idris is 3.

How many sheep do they each get?

G3 A box contains milk and plain chocolates in the ratio of 3 : 1.
The box contains 28 chocolates.

How many milk chocolates are in the box?

AQA 2003 Specimen

G4 A crumble contains blackberries and apples in the ratio 2 : 5.
The weight of the fruit altogether must weigh 350 g.

(a) What weight of blackberries should be used?

(b) What weight of apples should be used?

G5 The ratio of boys to girls in a sports club is 3 : 2.
If there are 60 members, how many are boys?

G6 Maize porridge is a popular food in Africa.
It is made from maize flour and water in the ratio 1:4.

How much maize flour and water is needed to make 750 g of porridge?

G7 Brass is made from copper and zinc in the ratio 4:1.

What weights of copper and zinc are needed to make 20 kg of brass?

G8 A judge rules that both Yukon Developments and Skelly Council are jointly responsible for a pollution disaster.
He orders that the £14 million costs be paid by Yukon and Skelly in the ratio 4:3.

How much do they each pay?

G9 A simple mixture of salt and sugar is added to water for use by aid workers in countries where there is a drought.
It is made from 1 part of salt and 8 parts of sugar.

How much salt and sugar are needed to make 450 kg of the mixture?

Ratios can be used where there are more than two quantities.
The ancient Chinese made gunpowder from: 5 parts of saltpetre
                                            1 part of sulphur
                                            2 parts of charcoal

This can be written as a ratio 5:1:2.

G10 Using the Chinese recipe for gunpowder above find what weights would be needed

(a) of saltpetre and charcoal with 50 g of sulphur

(b) of sulphur and charcoal with 100 g of saltpetre

(c) of all the ingredients to make 240 g of gunpowder.

G11 To make cheese straws you need flour, margarine and cheese in the ration 4:3:3.
Write out a recipe to make 500 g of cheese straw mix.

G12 A factory makes stainless steel using a mixture of iron, nickel and chromium in the ratio 3:1:1.

How much of each metal do they need to make up 80 kg of stainless steel?

Test yourself with these questions

T1 A recipe for chocolate mousse for 2 people uses these ingredients.

    100 g of chocolate
    10 g unsalted butter
    2 large eggs

(a) How much chocolate would be needed for 1 person?

(b) Write the ingredients needed for 6 people.

(c) John makes some mousse and uses 150 g chocolate.
How many people is he making the recipe for?
        OCR

T2 A 2 litre tin of paint covers 24 m^2 of wall.
How many litres of paint are needed to cover 60 m^2 of wall?

T3 (a) A DIY shop sells cement in two sizes:
    10 kg sack for £8.95   3 kg Handy-pack for £2.95
Which is the best value for money? Explain your answer.

(b) Varnish is sold in two sizes of tin
    200 ml for £4.65   500 ml for £11.95
Which is the best value for money? Explain your answer.

T4 George has £80.50 to share between his two nieces.
He decides to divide the money in the ratio of their ages.
Ann is 8 years old and Joan is 15 years old.

How much will Ann receive?
        AQA(NEAB) 1997

T5 Chocolate butter icing uses caster sugar, butter and
cocoa powder in the ratio 5 : 3 : 1.

(a) How much of each ingredient would you need to make 450 g of icing?

(b) If you used 100 g of caster sugar, how much butter would you need?

10 Metric measures

You will revise
- how to estimate lengths
- how to change feet into metres, miles into kilometres and pounds into kilograms

You will learn
- how to choose the right measurement to measure everyday objects
- how to change from pints and gallons into litres

A Estimating

A1 This book is roughly 20 cm wide.
Use this to estimate in centimetres

(a) how wide your desk is (b) the height of this book

(c) your handspan (d) how high your chair seat is above the floor

A2 A bag of sugar weighs 1 kilogram.
Estimate the weight in kilograms of

(a) your school bag (b) your chair (c) a pile of class exercise books

A3 A packet of 50 teabags usually weighs 125 grams.
Estimate the weight in grams of

(a) this book (b) a full pencil case (c) a ruler

A4 A large carton of orange juice contains 1 litre.
Estimate how much these contain in litres.

(a) your school bag (b) the rubbish bin in your classroom

A5 A normal teaspoon can hold about 5 ml (millilitres) of liquid
Estimate how many ml are in
(a) a small yoghurt pot   (b) a mug of tea   (c) a ballpoint pen

A6 What units would you use, mm, cm, m or km to measure
(a) the length of a lorry
(b) the distance from your class to the nearest beach
(c) the length of your foot
(d) the length of a fly

A7 A tonne is 1000 kilograms.
What units would you use, g, kg or tonne to estimate the weight of
(a) a large dog   (b) a hamster   (c) a van

A8 Write down the metric unit you would use to measure
(i) the length of a person's hand   (ii) the weight of a mouse
(iii) the distance from Manchester to London
(iv) a teaspoon of medicine.   Edexcel

A9 Change these lengths into centimetres
(a) 5 m   (b) 2.5 m   (c) 50 m
(d) 50 mm   (e) 200 mm   (f) 5 mm

A10 Change these lengths into metres
(a) 800 cm   (b) 150 cm   (c) 80 cm
(d) 7 km   (e) 25 km   (f) 0.75 km

A11 Change these weights into grams
(a) 2 kg   (b) 10 kg   (c) 0.5 kg   (d) $\frac{1}{4}$ kg

A12 Change these weights into kilograms
(a) 3000 g   (b) 1500 g   (c) 600 g   (d) 750 g

A13 Change these measurements
(a) 5 litres into ml   (b) 2.5 litres into ml   (c) 0.5 litres into ml
(d) 250 ml into litres   (e) 2000 ml into litres   (f) 1250 ml into litres

---

Have you got the bottle?

Wine bottles and other drinks are often labelled in 'cl'.
A normal wine bottle is given as 70 cl.
What does 'cl' mean?

B Liquid conversions

The metric measurement for liquids is a litre.
There are 1000 millilitres (ml) in one litre.

Things such as milk and beer are sometimes sold in pints.
A pint is slightly more than half a litre.
So a litre is roughly two pints.

Panic in the pub

Is beer drinking going to pot? Many regulars up and down the country are angry at what they see as the end of the traditional pint. EU plans to go metric would mean that the pint glass would become half a litre. This would mean that instead

B1 A milkman records how many pints he sells to some of his customers.
How many litres roughly are there in

(a) 8 pints (b) 20 pints
(c) 7 pints (d) 15 pints

B2 How many pints are there roughly in

(a) 6 litres (b) 15 litres (c) $2\frac{1}{2}$ litres (d) $12\frac{1}{2}$ litres

B3 Roughly how many millilitres are there in

(a) 1 pint (b) $\frac{1}{2}$ pint (c) $\frac{1}{4}$ pint (d) $\frac{3}{4}$ pint

B4 There are exactly 8 pints in a gallon.
A landlord records how many pints he sells of different beers in a week.

(a) Find how many pints he has used of each beer,
(b) Roughly how many litres of each beer has he sold?

| Witney's Pale | 12 gallons | Adlard's Old Socks | 4 gallons |
| Khronicberg | 15 gallons | Bugwiper | $8\frac{1}{2}$ gallons |

B5 A more accurate way of converting gallons into litres is to multiply by 4.5.
Use a calculator to change these amounts into litres

(a) 10 gallons (b) 5 gallons (c) $2\frac{1}{2}$ gallons
(d) 16 pints (e) 48 pints (f) 36 pints

Big hats?

Who says that everything in the US is bigger than the UK?
A US gallon is only 3.8 litres!

Cowboys often wear what is called a 'Ten-gallon' hat.

How many litres would 10 UK gallons be?

How many litres would 10 US gallons be?

C A mixed bag

There are roughly 2 pounds (lb) in 1 kilogram.

A foot is about 30 cm. (Look at a foot ruler!) So 3 feet are about one metre.

5 miles is very close to 8 km.

C1 Change these measurements into centimetres.

(a) 5 feet (b) 2 feet (c) 6 feet (d) 10 feet

C2 Change these measurements roughly into metres.

(a) 150 feet (b) 30 feet (c) 90 feet (d) 6000 feet

C3 Rewrite these sentences using metres.

(a) Our school swimming pool is 75 feet long.

(b) Our aeroplane flew at 12 000 feet.

(c) The peak of Mount Everest is nearly 30 000 feet above sea level.

(d) An Anaconda grows to about 20 feet in length.

(e) The highest waterfall in the world is Angel Falls in Venezuela and is 3000 feet high.

C4 Jenni's grandad has kept a record of how much he has weighed in pounds (lb) at different times of his life.
Copy and complete this table.

Age	Birth	10	30	50	80
Weight (lb)	8	56	164	220	185
Weight (kg)					

C5 These road signs are in miles.
Convert them into kilometres.

| Detford | 40 |
| Malpeth | 25 |

| Walford | 15 |
| Ardale | 50 |

| Midworth | 20 |
| Frotton | 10 |

C6 Fiona weighs 10 stone 3 pounds.

(a) There are 14 pounds in one stone.
Estimate her weight in kilograms.

Fiona is 5 feet 2 inches tall.

(b) There are 12 inches in one foot.
Take one inch as 2.5 centimetres.
Work out her height in metres.

OCR

Test yourself with these questions

T1 Give rough estimates in metric units for
   (a) the width of the back of your chair
   (b) the weight of your chair
   (c) the weight of a training shoe.

T2 Write down the **metric** unit you would use to measure
   (a) the weight of a car,
   (b) the distance from Birmingham to Glasgow,
   (c) the amount of lemonade in a glass,
   (d) the length of a bus.

   Edexcel

T3 Roughly how many litres are there in
   (a) 4 pints   (b) 10 pints   (c) 5 gallons

T4 Rewrite these statements using metric units
   (a) My Gran lives at Crumford which is about 35 miles away.
   (b) Heavyweight boxers must weigh over 190 pounds.
   (c) The current long jump record is nearly 30 feet

T5 (a) Roughly how many pints of milk does this container hold?

   (b) Roughly how many kilograms of rice does this bag of rice contain?

OCR

11 Looking at data 1

You will revise
- how to read information from tables including two way tables
- how to draw and interpret bar graphs and line graphs

You will learn
- about time series graphs and index numbers

A Reading tables

Boys' names

This table shows the most popular boys' names for new born babies in recent years:

Order	Year					
	1954	1964	1974	1984	1994	1999
1	David	David	Paul	Christopher	Thomas	Jack
2	John	Paul	Mark	James	James	Thomas
3	Stephen	Andrew	David	David	Jack	James
4	Michael	Mark	Andrew	Daniel	Daniel	Joshua
5	Peter	John	Richard	Michael	Matthew	Daniel

© Crown Copyright 2001 Source: National Statistics

A1 What was the most popular boys' name in 1984?

A2 Which name was the fourth most popular in 1964?

A3 Which name appears in the lists for the most number of years?

A4 Were any names amongst the five most popular in 1954 **and** in 1999?

On the buses

This is a timetable showing when buses leave a village bus stop.

Route	Times					
3	0830	1015	1230	1400	1620	1730
7	0745	0820	1125	1350	1845	
10	0925	1310	1525	1745	1900	
14	1020	1430	1635	2010		
28	0750	0940	1145	1535	1820	

A5 Which route has the most number of buses in a day?

A6 How many buses leave the stop after 4.30 p.m.?

A7 How many buses leave the stop between 9 in the morning and midday?

A8 Josh arrives at the bus stop at 1050.
  (a) What number is the first to arrive?
  (b) How long will he have to wait for this bus?

Home entertainment

A recent survey looked at what home entertainment facilities young people had in their bedrooms. The results were:

Type	Boys %	Girls %
Television	58	47
Games console	38	17
Video recorder	18	10
Computer	10	4
Satellite/cable	4	3
None of these	36	49

A9 What percentage of boys have a games console in their bedrooms?

A10 What percentage of girls **do not** have a video recorder in their bedroom?

A11 Which of these statements are supported by this data? Write true or false.

(a) *More than half of all girls have a television in their bedroom.*

(b) *More than twice as many boys have games consoles in their rooms as girls.*

(c) *Just under half of all girls had no home entertainment in their rooms.*

In the post

The cost of sending a letter in the UK is given in this table:

Weight up to	First Class	Second Class	Weight up to	First Class	Second Class
60 g	27p	19p	450 g	£1.41	£1.14
100 g	41p	33p	500 g	£1.58	£1.30
150 g	57p	44p	600 g	£1.90	£1.52
200 g	72p	54p	700 g	£2.39	£1.74
250 g	84p	66p	750 g	£2.56	£1.85*
300 g	96p	76p	800 g	£2.77	
350 g	£1.09	87p	900 g	£3.05	
400 g	£1.24	£1.00	**1000 g	£3.32	

* items heavier than 750 g cannot be sent by Second Class
** items heavier than 1000 g cost £3.32 plus 81p per 250 g or part thereof

A12 Find the cost of sending letters with these weights by first class post.

(a) 350 g (b) 525 g (c) 180 g (d) 1500 g

A13 What is the difference in cost between first and second class for a letter weighing

(a) 100 g (b) 380 g (c) 475 g (d) 680 g?

A14 Sadie has a large package to send which weighs 2 kg.
A private company will deliver it for £4.40.

How much cheaper is this than first class post?

B Two way tables

Elisa is a doing a survey on the type of houses in her area.
She surveys houses in the town and houses in the surrounding country.

	Type of house		
	Detached	Semi-det.	Terraced
Town	12	18	20
Country	8	10	7

> I think there are more detached houses in the town than there are in the country.

B1 Jake is doing a survey on how students get to school.
This table shows his results with some numbers missing.

	How they get to school			Total
	Walk/cycle	Bus	Car	
Boys	32	48		100
Girls	12		10	50
Total	44			150

(a) Copy and complete this table.

(b) What percentage of the boys in the survey walk or cycle to school?

(c) What percentage of the girls walk or cycle to school?

(d) Who in the survey are more likely to walk to school, boys or girls?

B2 (a) In Jake's survey who are more likely to use a bus to get to school, boys or girls? Give a reason for your answer.

(b) What can you say about the proportion of boys and girls who come to school by car?

B3 This table shows some results from a class survey.
Some of the numbers have been left out.

	Wear glasses	Don't wear glasses	Totals
Boys	5		13
Girls		10	
Totals	12		30

(a) Copy and complete this table.

(b) What fraction of boys wear glasses?

(c) How many girls were there altogether?

(d) What fraction of girls wear glasses?

B4 This table gives information about houses in a street.

	Garage	No Garage	Totals
Semi-detached houses	14		
Detached houses		2	
Totals	42	14	56

(a) How many detached houses have garages?

(b) How many detached houses are there in the street?

AQA(SEG) 1999

To write about the results in a two way table it is important to know the totals.
Before answering any questions about these tables it is useful
to add totals to the rows and columns.
Always add all the row totals and all the column totals to check you get the same overall total.

B5 These results are obtained for all the houses in a village.

	Number of bedrooms			
	2	3	4	5
Detached	0	10	8	2
Semi-detached	2	8	5	0
Terraced	10	15	0	0

(a) Copy this table and add row and column totals

(b) How many detached houses have 4 bedrooms?

(c) How many terraced houses are there?

(d) What percentage of detached houses have 3 bedrooms?

B6 This table shows the number of bedrooms and 'living' rooms for the houses in the village.

		Number of bedrooms			
		2	3	4	5
Number of living rooms	1	3	5	0	0
	2	9	20	0	1
	3	0	8	3	1

(a) How many houses had 2 living rooms?

(b) How many houses had 3 bedrooms and 3 living rooms

(c) How many houses had more living rooms than bedrooms?

B7 The two-way table shows the number of visits made to the doctor and the dentist by 80 college students in the summer term.

		Number of visits made to the doctor			
		0	1	2	3
Number of visits made to the dentist	0	24	10	2	1
	1	8	5	3	1
	2	10	7	0	0
	3	5	3	1	0

(a) How many students did **not** visit the doctor?

(b) How many students visited the dentist exactly 3 times?

(c) How many students made more visits to the doctor than they made to the dentist?

AQA(SEG) 2000

C Diagrams

This data shows the number of houses of different types in a small town.

Type of house	Detached	Bungalow	Semi-det.	Terraced	Flats
Number	60	15	122	97	53

Two ways we could present the data are a ...

pictogram or a .... bar chart

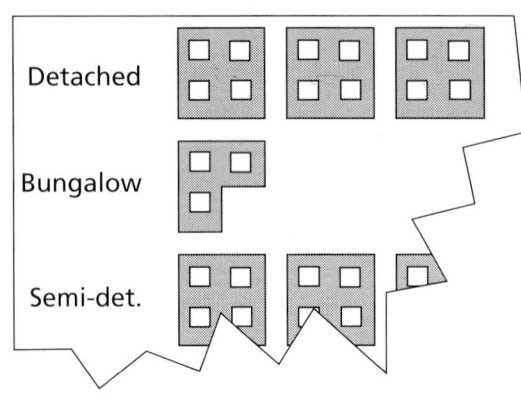
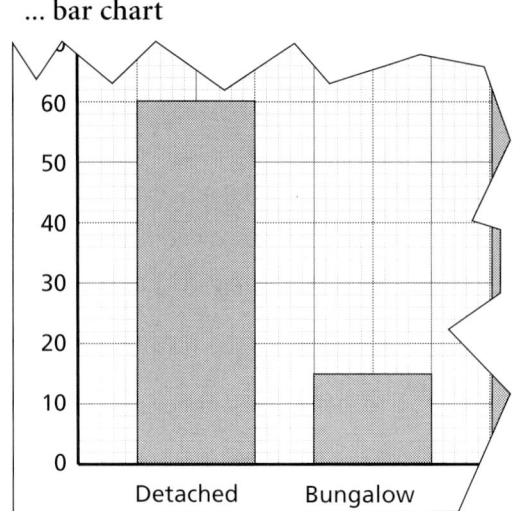

C1 Copy and complete the pictogram for the houses.
State clearly what one 'house' in the pictogram represents.

C2 Copy and complete the bar chart for the houses.

C3 This pictogram shows the number of parcels posted at the High Street Post Office on Monday, Tuesday and Wednesday.

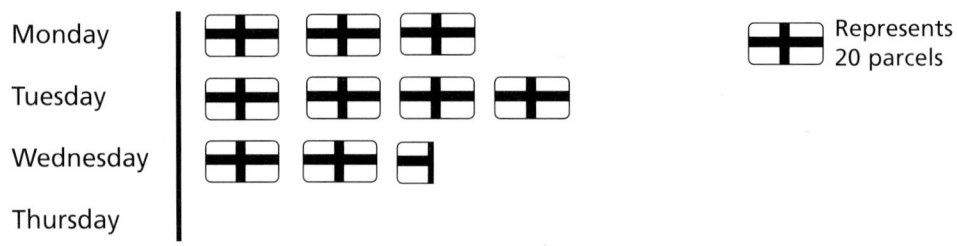

(a) How many parcels were posted on
  (i) Monday
  (ii) Wednesday?

25 parcels were posted on Thursday.

(b) Show this on a copy of the pictogram.

Edexcel

C4 Nasser has carried out a survey on the number of bedrooms in houses in his area. His results are shown in this bar chart.

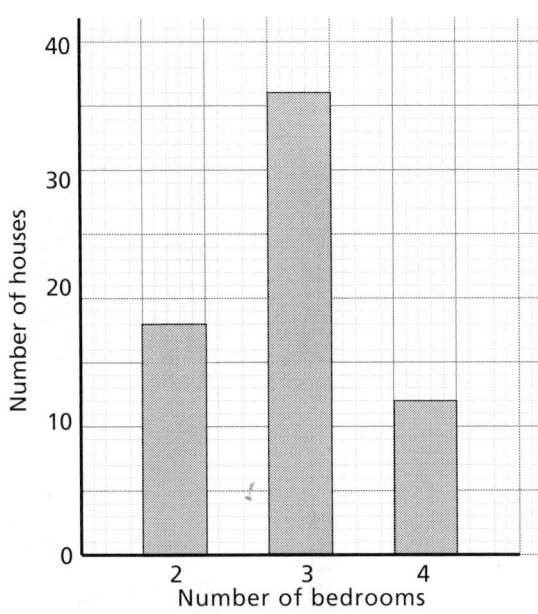

(a) What is the modal number of bedrooms in a house?

(b) How many houses did Nasser use in his survey?

(c) How many more 2 bedroom houses were there than 4 bedroom houses?

(d) How many bedrooms were there in all the houses surveyed together?

C5 Pat carried out a survey.
She asked each pupil in her class how many postcards they received last August. Her results are shown in the vertical line graph.

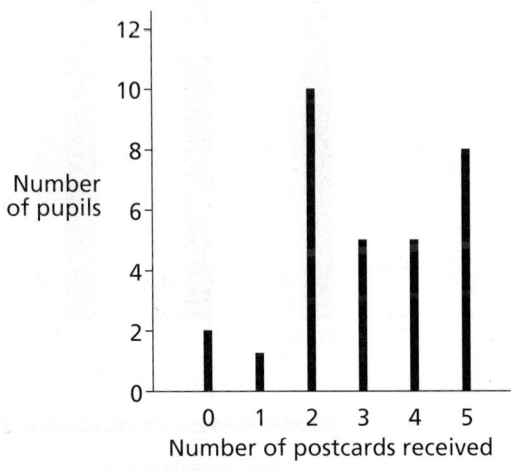

(a) What is the modal number of postcards received?

(b) How many pupils took part in the survey?

(c) How many postcards were received altogether?

AQA 1999

C6 A number of students were asked how many times they had used the canteen that week. The results were

Number of visits	0	1	2	3	4	5
Students	10	24	18	15	8	32

(a) Draw a suitable diagram for this data.

(b) Explain why you chose this type of diagram

D Composite bar charts

When you have more than one set of data it can be useful to show these side by side on a graph.

This data shows the number of different types of houses in a town and the surrounding country.

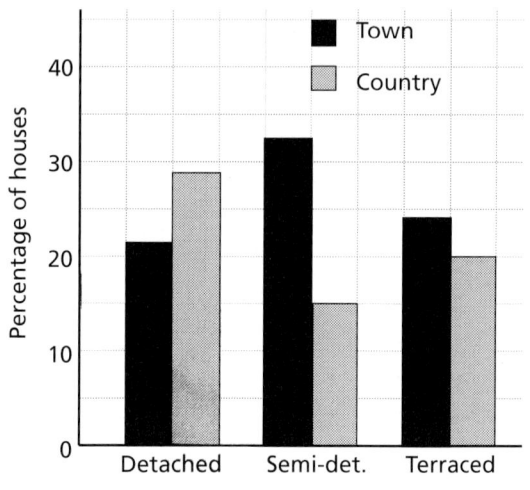

D1 (a) What is the modal type of house in the town?

(b) What is the modal type of house in the country?

D2 Which of the types of house did the survey show was more common in the town than in the country?

D3 This diagram shows the number of people in our armed forces between 1968 and 1998.

(a) Over the thirty years were the numbers in the armed forces going up, going down or staying about the same?

(b) Which was the biggest of the armed forces in 1968?
Was is it still biggest in 1998?

(c) Between what years does the chart show that the numbers in the Air Force increase?

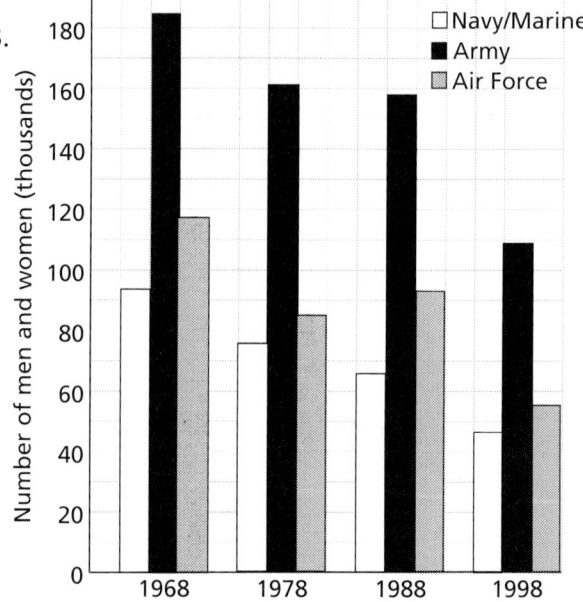

D4 A survey was conducted to find out which activities 11-year old pupils do after school. The results are displayed here.

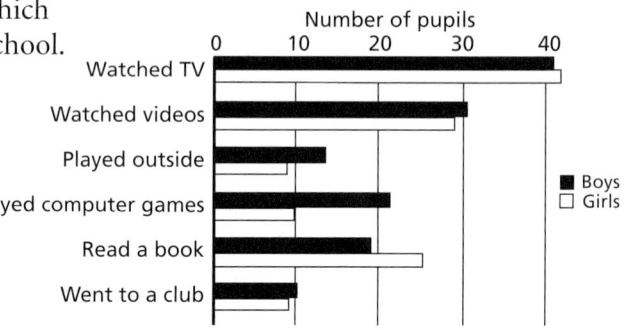

(a) Which activity was chosen most often by boys and girls?

(b) The survey shows that after school, more boys played outside than girls.

Write down two other findings from the survey that tell us about the differences between

98 • *11 Looking at data 1*

E Line graphs

Line graphs are useful to show how something changes over a period of time.

This line graph shows the average amount of pocket money received by 6–9 year old children between 1989 and 1999.

A line graph with time on the *x*-axis is called a **time series graph**.

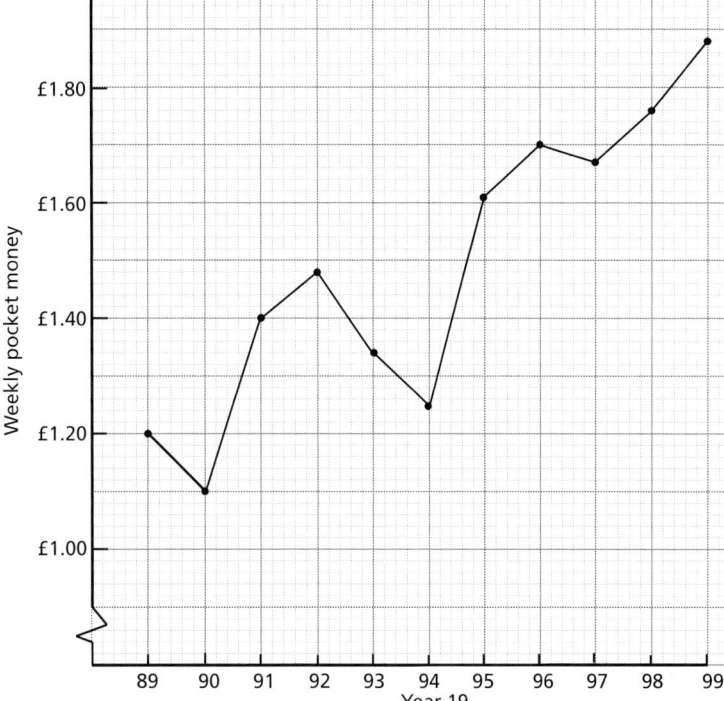

E1 Why has a jagged line been drawn at the bottom of the pocket money axis?

E2 What was the average amount of pocket money given to 6–9 year olds in
  (a) 1989   (b) 1994   (c) 1999

E3 (a) Between which two consecutive years did the amount of pocket money go up most?
  (b) Only once did the average amount go down for two consecutive years. Between which years was this?

E4 Which of these statements describes what the graph shows about 6–9 year olds' average pocket money?

  | It generally got less between 1989 and 1999 |

  | It generally went up between 1989 and 1999 |

  | It stayed about the same between 1989 and 1999 |

E5 This table shows the number of cinema tickets sold between 1986 and 1999.

Year	1986	1987	1988	1989	1990	1991	1992	1993	1994	1995	1996	1997	1998	1999
Tickets (millions)	73	75	78	88	89	93	98	113	124	115	123	139	135	139

  (a) Draw a line graph of these figures on sheet P131.
  (b) Make two statements about what the graph tells you about sales of cinema tickets.

E6 This graph shows the number of journeys made by passengers on British airlines each month.

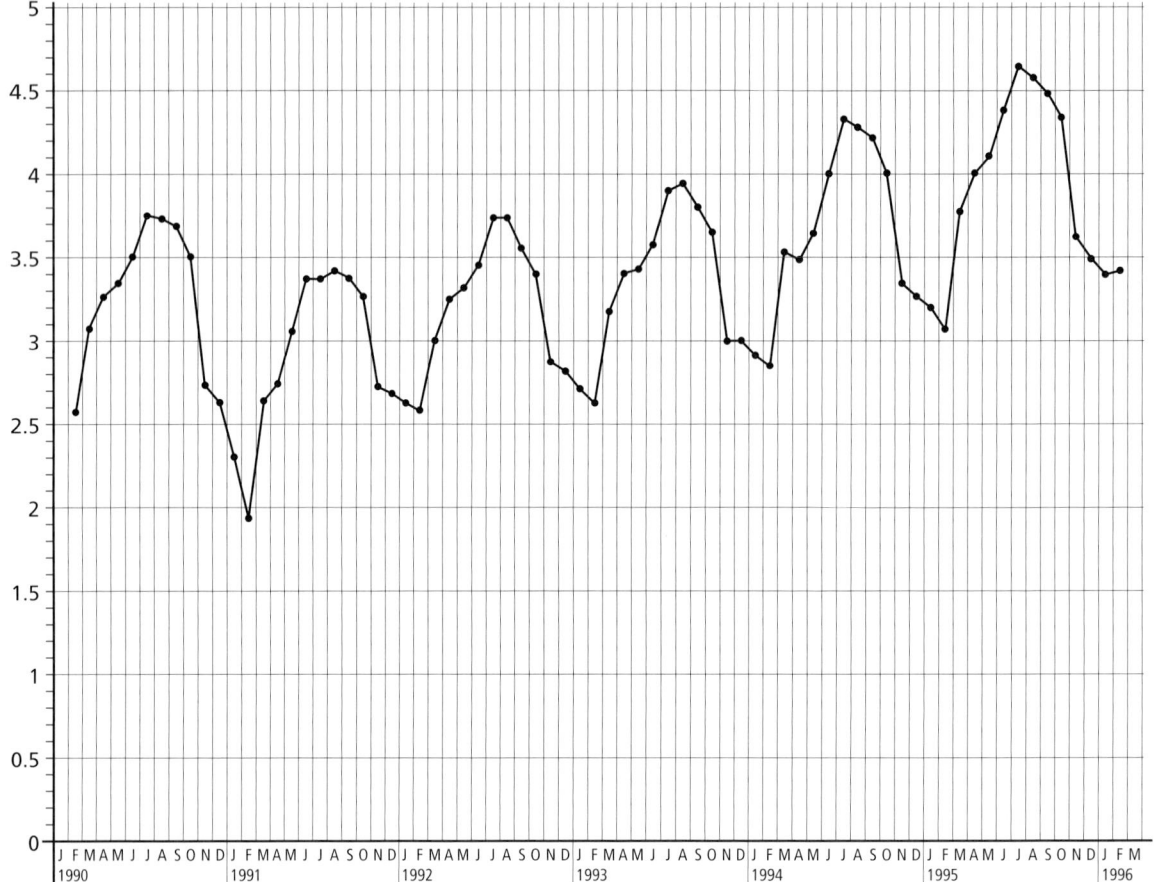

(a) What do the letters JFMAMJJASOND stand for?

(b) On the graph, which months are usually the busiest?

(c) Which month is usually the least busy?

(d) Between 1990 and 1996 did airline business generally get better, get worse or stay the same?

(e) Was there an unusual pattern in any of the years?

F Index numbers

When people want to look at how something changes over a period of time they sometimes use an **index number**.

A starting point in time is made to be 100% of an amount.

Any time following this the amount is written as a percentage of what it was at the start.

Year	Index of bird populations			
	1970	1980	1990	1998
Song thrush	100	67	51	45
Spotted flycatcher	100	105	55	32
Tree sparrow	100	74	17	13

In this table the population of birds was set at 100% in 1970.

In 1990 the population of the Song thrush was 51% of what it was in 1970.

F1 Answer these questions from the table above.

(a) What percentage of the 1970 population was the Spotted flycatcher population in 1998?

(b) Which bird saw the biggest percentage drop in population between 1970 and 1998.

(c) Which bird population actually increased between 1970 and 1980?

The Retail Price Index

The Government keeps a check on prices of goods in the UK.
Each month they check the prices of a wide range of things people spend money on.
This is recorded as an index called the **Retail Price Index (RPI)**.

The RPI was set at 100 in April 1987.
When the news talks about a rise in inflation they are talking about the RPI.

F2 This table shows the annual RPI from 1990 to 2000.

Year	1990	1991	1992	1993	1994	1995	1996	1997	1998	1999	2000
RPI	126	134	139	141	144	149	153	158	163	165	170

(a) By what percentage had the RPI increased from the start in 1987 to 1997?

(b) Draw a line graph of the RPI between 1990 and 1999 using these scales.

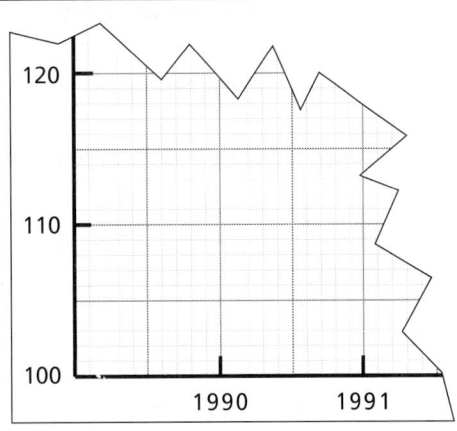

Test yourself with these questions

T1 This table shows the number of students who took examinations in four different subjects in 1997 and 1998.

Subject	Number of students 1997	Number of students 1998
Religious Studies	2860	3358
Law	4389	4617
German	2007	2481
Statistics	1999	2491

(a) Which of these subjects had the least number of students taking the exam in 1998?

(b) How many more students took the Statistics exam in 1998 than in 1997?

(c) Which of the subjects had the greatest increase in the number of students taking the exam from 1997 to 1998?

AQA(NEAB) 1999

T2 This table shows how a group of students travel to school.

	Car	Bus	Walk	Cycle
Boys	5	12	12	7
Girls	8	12	6	1

(a) How many boys were there in the group?

(b) What fraction of the boys walked to school?

(c) For this group which had the greater fraction of people who walked, boys or girls? Explain your answer.

T3 Jackie counted the number of cars passing different places in 30 minutes. The pictogram shows her results.

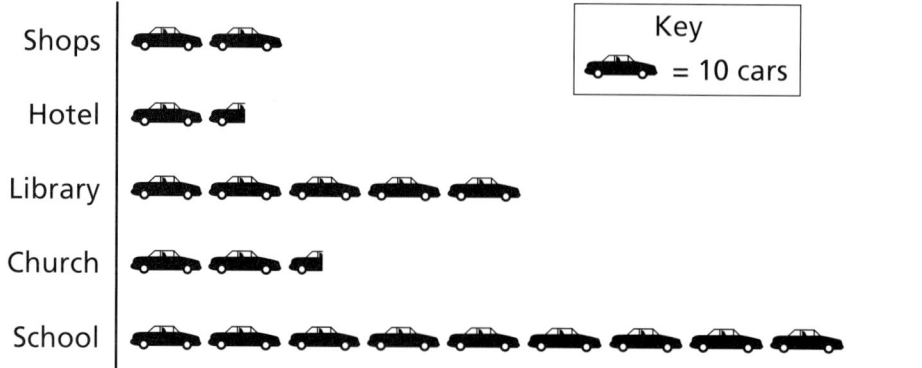

(a) How many cars passed the **school**? (b) How many cars passed the **church**?

(c) 20 cars passed the shops. Jackie counted 200 cars altogether.

What fraction of the cars passed the shops?
Give your answer in its simplest form.

AQA(SEG) 2000

T4 This bar chart shows which day of the week shoppers went to a supermarket in 1994 and 1996.

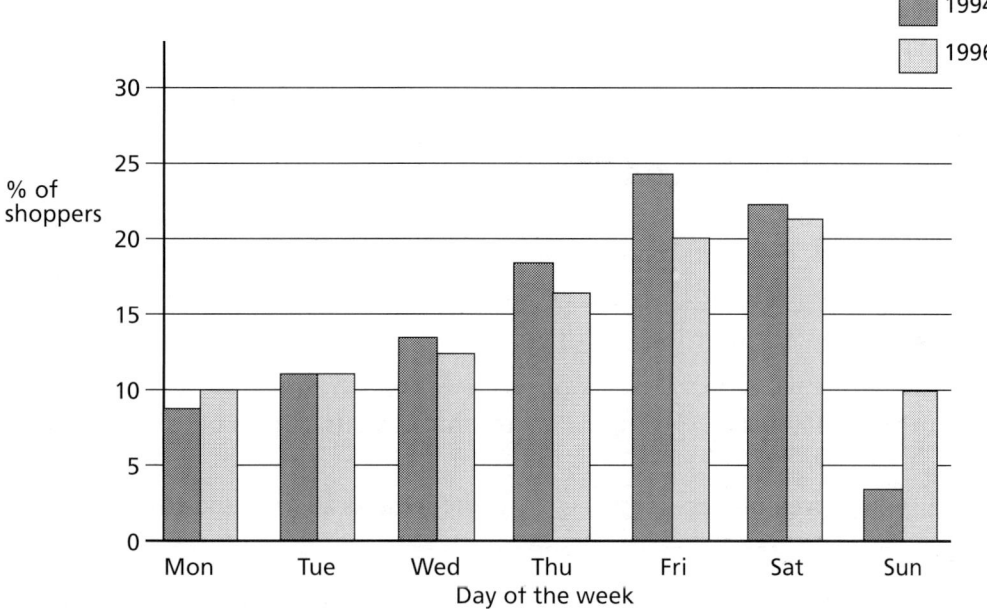

(a) Which day of the week was the most popular day for shopping in 1994?

(b) Did the shoppers choose different days for shopping in 1996 compared with 1994? Give a reason for your answer.

(c) 'In 1996, about half the shoppers did their shopping at the end of the week (Friday, Saturday and Sunday).'

Is this statement true or false?
Show all your working.

AQA(SEG) 1998

T5 This table shows the heating costs for Sam's house for six months.

Month	Jan	Feb	March	April	May	June
Cost (£)	35	40	30	20	15	10

(a) Draw a line graph of this data on sheet P132.

(b) Why do you think that June had the lowest heating costs?

AQA(SEG) 2000

12 Negative numbers 2

You will revise adding and subtracting negative numbers
You will learn how to multiply and divide negative numbers

A Adding and subtracting

A1 Work these out.
(a) $2 - 7$ (b) $^-2 + 5$ (c) $1 - 5$ (d) $^-3 + 9$ (e) $^-3 + 3$
(f) $^-1 - 3$ (g) $^-2 - 8$ (h) $0 - 4$ (i) $^-3 - 10$ (j) $^-5 - 4$

> Adding a negative number ... $(2 + ^-6)$ ... is the same as subtracting a positive number $(2 - 6)$
>
> Subtracting a negative number ... $(2 - ^-6)$ ... is the same as adding a positive number $(2 + 6)$

A2 Work these out.
(a) $5 + ^-2$ (b) $2 + ^-5$ (c) $6 + ^-6$ (d) $^-7 + ^-3$
(e) $^-1 + ^-9$ (f) $^-2 + ^-1 + ^-3$ (g) $^-3 + ^-3 + ^-3$ (h) $^-7 + 3 + ^-1$

A3 Find the missing number in each calculation.
(a) $5 + \blacksquare = 4$ (b) $3 + \blacksquare = ^-4$ (c) $^-6 + \blacksquare = 2$
(d) $\blacksquare + ^-2 = ^-5$ (e) $6 + \blacksquare = ^-3$ (f) $\blacksquare + ^-8 = ^-9$

A4 In a magic square the numbers in each **row**, each **column** and each **diagonal** add to the **same total**.

Copy and complete these magic squares.

(a) 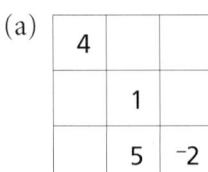 (b) 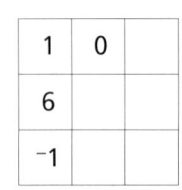 (c) 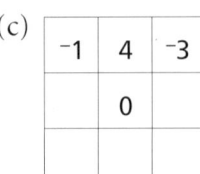 (d)

A5 Work these out.
(a) $3 - ^-2$ (b) $1 - ^-9$ (c) $6 - ^-4$ (d) $1 - ^-6$ (e) $^-1 - ^-6$
(f) $^-2 - ^-5$ (g) $^-3 - ^-3$ (h) $^-10 - ^-4$ (i) $^-8 - ^-1$ (j) $^-7 - ^-4$

A6 Work these out.
(a) $2 - 5$ (b) $^-3 + 8$ (c) $^-6 - 3$ (d) $^-4 + ^-7$ (e) $1 - ^-3$
(f) $4 - ^-5$ (g) $^-2 + ^-6$ (h) $^-1 - ^-7$ (i) $0 - ^-5$ (j) $^-9 - ^-7$

A7 Choose pairs of numbers from the loop to make these calculations correct.

(a) ☐ − ☐ = ⁻4   (b) ☐ + ☐ = ⁻5
(c) ☐ + ☐ = ⁻4   (d) ☐ − ☐ = ⁻6
(e) ☐ − ☐ = 8   (f) ☐ + ☐ = ⁻10

Loop: ⁻5, ⁻3, 6, 4, 2, 1, ⁻7

*A8 Use two numbers from 7, 2, ⁻5, ⁻8 and either + or − to get the following results.

(a) ⁻13   (b) ⁻6   (c) ⁻5   (d) ⁻10   (e) 12

B *Multiplying*

- Match the expressions on the left with the expressions on the right.
- Can you work out the answer to each multiplication?

A ⁻2 + ⁻2
B 0 + 0
C ⁻4 + ⁻4 + ⁻4
D ⁻2 + ⁻2 + ⁻2 + ⁻2 + ⁻2

P ⁻2 × 5
Q 2 × ⁻2
R 3 × ⁻4
S 2 × 0

- Can you continue these patterns?

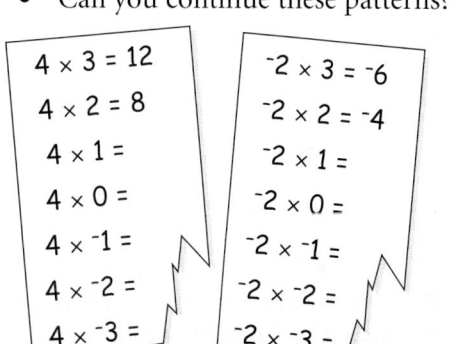

4 × 3 = 12
4 × 2 = 8
4 × 1 =
4 × 0 =
4 × ⁻1 =
4 × ⁻2 =
4 × ⁻3 =

⁻2 × 3 = ⁻6
⁻2 × 2 = ⁻4
⁻2 × 1 =
⁻2 × 0 =
⁻2 × ⁻1 =
⁻2 × ⁻2 =
⁻2 × ⁻3 =

- Can you complete this multiplication grid, shown on sheet P133?

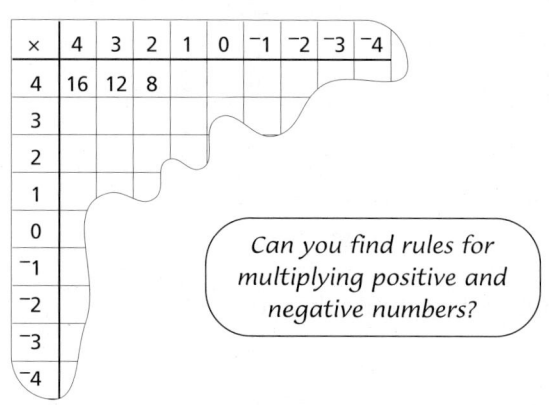

Can you find rules for multiplying positive and negative numbers?

B1 Write down the answers to these.

(a) 4 × ⁻3   (b) ⁻3 × 2   (c) 3 × ⁻3   (d) ⁻4 × 0   (e) 4 × ⁻1
(f) ⁻2 × ⁻3   (g) ⁻4 × ⁻3   (h) 1 × 4   (i) ⁻3 × ⁻3   (j) ⁻2 × ⁻4

Rules for multiplying positive and negative numbers

- negative × positive ⟶ negative ⟵ positive × negative
  - ⁻5 × 4 = ⁻20
  - 5 × ⁻4 = ⁻20

- positive × positive ⟶ positive ⟵ negative × negative
  - 5 × 4 = 20
  - ⁻5 × ⁻4 = 20

B2 Calculate these.
  (a) 6 × ⁻4 (b) ⁻5 × ⁻3 (c) ⁻2 × 5 (d) 3 × 7 (e) ⁻3 × 7
  (f) ⁻3 × ⁻7 (g) 3 × ⁻7 (h) 2 × 6 × ⁻3 (i) ⁻5 × ⁻7 × 2 (j) ⁻4 × ⁻1 × ⁻2

B3 Copy and complete these multiplication grids.

(a)
×	4	⁻3	2
5	20	⁻15	
⁻2			
⁻4			

(b)
×	⁻10	8	⁻4
⁻5	50		
6		⁻60	
⁻1			

B4 This is a 'multiplication wall'.

The number on each brick is found by multiplying the two numbers on the bricks below.

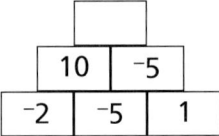

What will be the number on the top brick of this wall?

B5 Copy and complete these 'multiplication walls'.

(a) 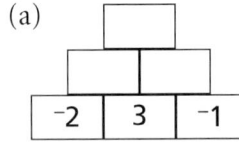   (b) 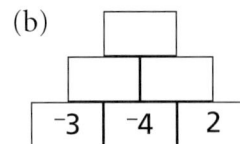   (c)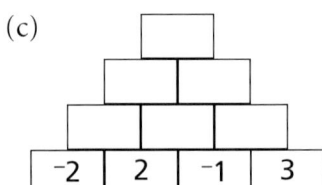

B6 Find the missing number in each calculation.
  (a) 5 × ■ = ⁻30 (b) ⁻4 × ■ = ⁻28 (c) ■ × ⁻3 = 15 (d) ■ × ⁻4 = 24

B7 Copy and complete these 'multiplication walls'.

(a) 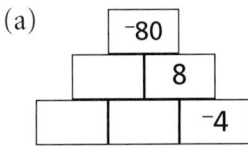   (b) 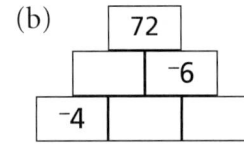   (c)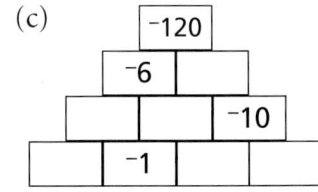

B8 (a) Copy and complete $(^-5)^2 = ^-5 \times {}^-5 = \ldots$

(b) Work out (i) $(^-3)^2$ (ii) $(^-4)^2$ (iii) $(^-6)^2$

B9 Copy and complete these multiplication grids.

(a)
×	5	⁻3
	10	
⁻3	⁻15	

(b)
×		5	
		⁻15	
⁻1	5		⁻6
	⁻20	20	

(c)
×			
	1		⁻2
⁻4	12	0	
			⁻10

*__B10__ In this grid each letter corresponds to a number.

For example K corresponds to 20 because 5 × 4 = 20.

×	2	⁻3	4	⁻6
⁻2	A	B	C	D
⁻3	E	F	G	H
5	I	J	K	L
⁻5	M	N	O	P

(a) What number corresponds to the letter J?

(b) What letter corresponds to the number ⁻10?

(c) For each set of numbers, work out the corresponding letters to spell a word.

  (i) 30, ⁻4, ⁻8, 20   (ii) 9, 10, 15, 12   (iii) ⁻12, ⁻30, ⁻20, 6, ⁻6

*__B11__ Do the multiplication wall puzzles on sheet P134.

C Dividing

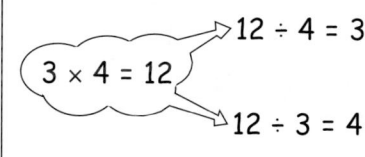 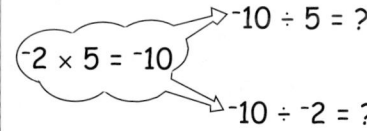 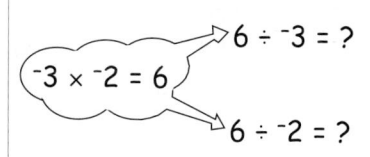

C1 Work these out.

(a) $12 \div {}^-2$ (b) $^-8 \div 4$ (c) $^-6 \div {}^-3$ (d) $^-14 \div {}^-2$

(e) $20 \div {}^-5$ (f) $^-30 \div 10$ (g) $^-15 \div {}^-5$ (h) $^-16 \div {}^-8$

C2 Find the missing number in each calculation.

(a) $30 \div \blacksquare = {}^-15$ (b) $^-20 \div \blacksquare = {}^-4$ (c) $\blacksquare \div {}^-3 = 4$

(d) $\blacksquare \div {}^-4 = 6$ (e) $^-25 \div \blacksquare = 5$ (f) $\blacksquare \div {}^-6 = {}^-3$

C3 Choose pairs of numbers from the loop to make these calculations correct.

(a) $\square \div \square = {}^-3$ (b) $\square \div \square = 2$

(c) $\square \div \square = 4$ (d) $\square \div \square = {}^-5$

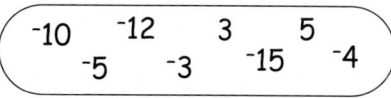

Rules for dividing positive and negative numbers

- negative ÷ positive   ⟶ negative $^-20 ÷ 4 = {}^-5$
- positive ÷ negative   ⟶ negative $20 ÷ {}^-4 = {}^-5$

- positive ÷ positive   ⟶ positive $20 ÷ 4 = 5$
- negative ÷ negative   ⟶ positive $^-20 ÷ {}^-4 = 5$

C4 Calculate these.
(a) $5 × {}^-2$ (b) $^-20 ÷ {}^-10$ (c) $^-30 ÷ 6$ (d) $^-4 × {}^-8$ (e) $^-5 × 8$
(f) $^-35 ÷ {}^-5$ (g) $6 × {}^-4$ (h) $18 ÷ {}^-9$ (i) $^-25 ÷ {}^-5$ (j) $^-7 × {}^-9$

C5 Find the missing number in each calculation.
(a) $7 × \blacksquare = {}^-28$ (b) $^-5 × \blacksquare = 30$ (c) $\blacksquare ÷ 2 = {}^-6$
(d) $\blacksquare × 4 = {}^-16$ (e) $\blacksquare ÷ {}^-7 = {}^-2$ (f) $\blacksquare × {}^-4 = {}^-40$
(g) $\blacksquare × {}^-9 = {}^-27$ (h) $^-45 ÷ \blacksquare = 9$ (i) $24 ÷ \blacksquare = {}^-3$

C6 Here is a number machine chain.

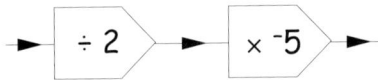

Find the output for each of these inputs.
(a) 10   (b) $^-8$ (c) $^-2$

C7 Choose pairs of numbers from the loop to make these calculations correct.
(a) ☐ ÷ ☐ = $^-3$ (b) ☐ × ☐ = 14
(c) ☐ × ☐ = $^-6$ (d) ☐ ÷ ☐ = $^-5$
(e) ☐ ÷ ☐ = 5   (f) ☐ × ☐ = $^-63$

$^-7$ $^-3$ 3 10
7 $^-2$ 21 $^-10$

C8 Use two numbers from $6, {}^-15, 3, {}^-3$ and either × or ÷ to get the following results.
(a) 2   (b) $^-2$ (c) $^-9$ (d) 45   (e) 5

C9 Use two numbers from $12, {}^-12, 3, {}^-6$ and either × or ÷ to get the following results.
(a) 2   (b) 72   (c) $^-4$ (d) $^-2$ (e) $^-36$

*****C10** Here is a number machine chain.

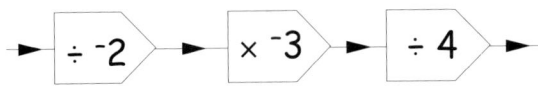

(a) Find the output for an input of $^-16$.
(b) Which input gives an output of 9?

D Mixed calculations

D1 Work these out.
(a) $3 + {}^-10$ (b) $5 \times {}^-6$ (c) $5 - 9$ (d) $10 \div {}^-2$ (e) ${}^-7 + {}^-2$
(f) ${}^-4 \times {}^-5$ (g) ${}^-16 \div 8$ (h) $({}^-10)^2$ (i) ${}^-12 \div {}^-6$ (j) $6 - {}^-1$

D2 Work these out.
(a) $2 + {}^-6 + {}^-3$ (b) $2 - 3 - 4$ (c) $3 \times {}^-2 \times {}^-4$ (d) ${}^-3 \times {}^-2 \times {}^-7$

D3 Calculate these.
(a) $(2 + {}^-3) \times 5$ (b) $4 \times (2 - 9)$ (c) $(1 - 4)^2$ (d) $({}^-1 + {}^-4) \times {}^-3$
(e) $\dfrac{{}^-1 + {}^-5}{2}$ (f) $\dfrac{3 \times {}^-6}{9}$ (g) $\dfrac{2 - 11}{{}^-3}$ (h) $\dfrac{({}^-6)^2}{{}^-9}$

D4 Find the missing number in each calculation.
(a) $6 - \blacksquare = {}^-4$ (b) $\blacksquare \times {}^-3 = 27$ (c) $\blacksquare \div 5 = {}^-4$
(d) $2 + \blacksquare + {}^-4 = {}^-3$ (e) ${}^-2 \times \blacksquare = {}^-18$ (f) ${}^-24 \div \blacksquare = 3$

D5 This table shows the lowest temperatures each day for a week in Glasgow in winter.

Day	Mon	Tues	Wed	Thur	Fri	Sat	Sun
Temperature (°C)	${}^-7$	3	${}^-6$	2	${}^-3$	${}^-7$	3

(a) Which days of the week were coldest?
(b) What was the difference between the highest and lowest temperatures in the table?
(c) Calculate the mean of the temperatures in the table.

D6 A sequence begins $2, {}^-6, 10, {}^-22, \ldots$

A rule to continue this sequence is,

add 1 to the last number and then multiply by ${}^-2$.

What are the next two numbers in this sequence?

D7 Here is a number machine chain.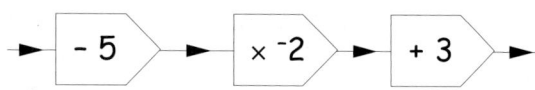

Find the output for each of these inputs.
(a) 8 (b) 1 (c) ${}^-5$

D8 (a) Copy and complete the boxes.
(i) $\square \times \square = \boxed{-10}$ (ii) $\square \div \square = \boxed{-1}$

(b) Work out $\dfrac{(-7) \times (-7) \times (+8)}{(-2)}$

AQA(NEAB) 1998

*D9 Use two numbers from $6, 9, {}^-2, {}^-10$ and either $+, -, \times$ or $\div$ to get the following results.
(a) ${}^-4$ (b) ${}^-11$ (c) 16 (d) ${}^-18$ (e) 5

E Substitution

What is the value of each expression when $a = {}^-2$ and $b = {}^-6$?

$a + b$
$a + b = {}^-2 + {}^-6$
$= {}^-8$

$b^2 + a$
$b^2 + a = ({}^-6)^2 + {}^-2$
$= {}^-6 \times {}^-6 + {}^-2$
$= 36 + {}^-2$
$= 34$

$ab + 5$
$ab + 5 = {}^-2 \times {}^-6 + 5$
$= 12 + 5$
$= 17$

$\frac{b}{a} - 1$
$\frac{b}{a} - 1 = \frac{{}^-6}{{}^-2} - 1$
$= 3 - 1$
$= 2$

E1 Work out the value of each expression when $p = {}^-4$ and $q = {}^-3$.
(a) $p + 5$
(b) $q - 1$
(c) $2p - 3$
(d) $3q + 10$
(e) $\frac{p}{2}$

E2 What is the value of each expression when $a = 6$ and $b = {}^-2$?
(a) $a + b$
(b) ab
(c) $b - a$
(d) $\frac{a}{b}$
(e) $a - b$

E3 Work out the value of each expression when $m = {}^-4$ and $n = {}^-2$.
(a) $2n + 5$
(b) $3m + 1$
(c) m^2
(d) $n^2 - 5$
(e) $\frac{3m}{2}$

E4 What is the value of each expression when $x = {}^-10$, $y = 5$ and $z = {}^-2$?
(a) $2x + y$
(b) $xz + 3$
(c) $x + 2y$
(d) $y - z$
(e) $3y + 2z$

E5 Work out the value of each expression when $a = {}^-3$, $b = 9$ and $c = {}^-6$.
(a) $a^2 + c$
(b) $2b - c$
(c) $\frac{c^2}{a}$
(d) $2ac$
(e) $\frac{2c}{a}$

E6 Do the puzzles on sheet P135.

E7 Work out the values of each expression below when $a = {}^-6$, $b = 4$ and $c = {}^-3$.
Use the code below to change the values to letters.
Rearrange each set of letters to spell a boy's name.

(a) $c + 3$, $b + c$, $a + b$, $2(c + 1)$

(b) $a + b + c$, $c^2 - 14$, $\frac{a^2}{9}$, $\frac{a}{c}$

(c) $a + 6$, $\frac{c}{3}$, $\frac{a}{c} + 1$, $a - c$, $\frac{b - c}{7}$

(d) $2c + 7$, $3c + 5$, $2a + b - c$, $c + 1$, $\frac{ac}{6}$, $\frac{4c}{a}$

(e) $2b + a$, $5c + 11$, $a - 2c$, $a + 1$, $4(b + c)$, $a + 9$, $3c + b$

Code

E	H	I	J	M	N	O	P	S	T
-5	-4	-3	-2	-1	0	1	2	3	4

E8 A rough formula for conversion of temperatures is:

$$F = 2C + 30$$

where C is the temperature in °C
and F is the temperature is °F.

What is the value of F when
(a) $C = 10$
(b) $C = {}^-11$
(c) $C = {}^-15$
(d) $C = {}^-18$

Test yourself with these questions

T1 Calculate these.
(a) $3 \times {}^-4$
(b) ${}^-5 \times 5$
(c) ${}^-6 \times {}^-3$
(d) $({}^-5)^2$
(e) ${}^-3 \times {}^-2 \times 4$

T2 Calculate these.
(a) ${}^-12 \div 4$
(b) ${}^-8 \div {}^-4$
(c) $14 \div {}^-7$
(d) ${}^-18 \div {}^-2$
(e) ${}^-36 \div 9$

T3 Calculate these.
(a) ${}^-6 \times {}^-3$
(b) ${}^-6 \div {}^-3$
(c) ${}^-12 \times 2$
(d) ${}^-12 \div 2$
(e) ${}^-2 \times {}^-3 \times {}^-1$

T4 Find the missing number in each calculation.
(a) $3 \times \blacksquare = {}^-24$
(b) ${}^-2 \times \blacksquare = 12$
(c) $\blacksquare \div 3 = {}^-4$
(d) $\blacksquare \div {}^-3 = 5$
(e) $15 \div \blacksquare = {}^-5$
(f) $\blacksquare \times {}^-6 = {}^-18$

T5 Calculate these.
(a) $2 + {}^-4$
(b) ${}^-2 - 5$
(c) $1 - {}^-4$
(d) ${}^-2 - {}^-5$
(e) ${}^-10 + 8$

T6 Choose pairs of numbers from the loop to make these calculations correct.
(a) $\square + \square = {}^-6$
(b) $\square \times \square = {}^-15$
(c) $\square - \square = {}^-8$
(d) $\square \div \square = {}^-4$
(e) $\square + \square = {}^-13$
(f) $\square \times \square = 40$

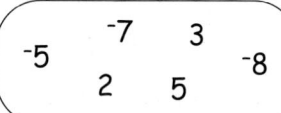

$^-7 \quad 3$
$^-5 \quad \quad \quad ^-8$
$2 \quad 5$

T7 Calculate these.
(a) $(1 - 4) \times {}^-2$
(b) $\dfrac{{}^-2 + {}^-7}{{}^-3}$
(c) ${}^-4 \times (1 - {}^-3)$
(d) $\dfrac{{}^-1 \times {}^-5 \times 6}{2}$

T8 Work out the value of each expression when $x = 2$, $y = {}^-3$ and $z = {}^-4$.
(a) $z + 1$
(b) $3x - 8$
(c) y^2
(d) xz
(e) yz
(f) $2x + 3y$
(g) $\dfrac{z}{x}$
(h) $5x - y$
(i) $\dfrac{2(y + z)}{7}$
(j) $z^2 + x$

T9 $P = ab + b^2$

Work out the value of P when $a = 4$, $b = {}^-5$.

OCR

13 Percentage calculations 1

You will revise
- how to change between fractions and percentages

You will learn how to
- find percentages of different amounts
- write one number as a percentage of another

A Fractions and percentages

A1 Some of these signs mean the same thing.
  (a) Match up the pairs that say the same thing.
  (b) Make a sign to match up with the odd one out.

A2 Write these fractions as percentages.
  (a) $\frac{89}{100}$ (b) $\frac{7}{100}$ (c) $\frac{1}{2}$ (d) $\frac{1}{4}$
  (e) $\frac{3}{4}$ (f) $\frac{1}{10}$ (g) $\frac{7}{10}$ (h) $\frac{2}{5}$

A3 Write these percentages as fractions.
  Simplify them if possible.
  (a) 37%   (b) 9%   (c) 25%   (d) 30%
  (e) 20%   (f) 85%   (g) 16%   (h) 15%

A4 Copy and complete these statements.
  (a) $\frac{3}{50} = \frac{}{100} = \%$ (b) $\frac{12}{25} = \frac{}{100} = \%$
  (c) $\frac{68}{200} = \frac{}{100} = \%$ (d) $\frac{150}{200} = \frac{}{100} = \%$
  (e) $\frac{7}{20} = \frac{}{100} = \%$ (f) $\frac{27}{50} = \frac{}{100} = \%$

B In your head

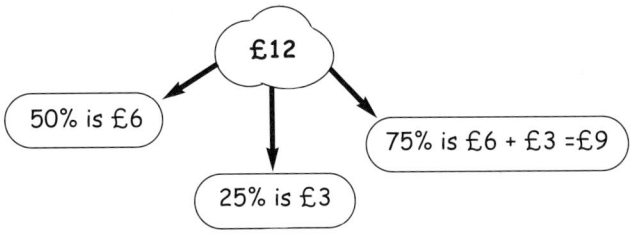

Useful facts

50% is the same as $\frac{1}{2}$

25% is the same as $\frac{1}{4}$

75% is 50% + 25% and is the same as $\frac{3}{4}$

B1 Work out 50% of
(a) £40 (b) 84p (c) 30 kg (d) 200 ml (e) 70 litres

B2 Work out 25% of
(a) £16 (b) 40 kg (c) 64p (d) 500 g (e) 30 cm

B3 Work out 75% of
(a) £20 (b) 80 kg (c) 200 ml (d) 24p (e) 18 m

B4 Work out
(a) 50% of £50 (b) 25% of 36 kg (c) 75% of 60 pens (d) 75% of 160 g

B5 Sanjay earns 25% commission on every secondhand car he sells. How much will he earn on selling these cars?
(a) Ford Fiesta £500 (b) Jeep £8000 (c) Skoda £1800

10% is the same as $\frac{1}{10}$.
To work out 10% of something – divide by 10.

10% of 80 = 80 ÷ 10 = 8

Once you know what 10% is you can easily work out 20%, 30% ....

20% of 80 = 2 × 8 = 16

60% of 80 = 6 × 8 = 48

B6 Work out 10% of
(a) £70 (b) 300 ml (c) 150 g (d) 50 litres (e) £8.50

B7 Work out
(a) 10% of £60 (b) 20% of £60 (c) 90% of £60 (d) 40% of £60

B8 Work out
(a) 20% of £90 (b) 70% of 30 kg (c) 10% of 120 g (d) 60% of 80 g

B9 How much **extra** do you get in these offers.
(a) a 200 g tube of tomato puree with 30% extra
(b) a 250 g bag of pasta with 20% extra
(c) a 750 ml bottle of wine with 10% extra.

> 5% is half of 10%
>
> 10% of 80 = 8
>
> 5% of 80 = 8 ÷ 2 = 4
>
> This helps to work out other percentages
>
> 30% of 80 = 3 × 8 = 24
>
> so 35% of 80 = 24 + 4 = 28

B10 Work out

(a) 10% of £40 (b) 5% of £40 (c) 15% of £40 (d) 35% of £40

B11 Work out

(a) 10% of 120 g (b) 5% of 120 g (c) 35% of 120 g (d) 85% of 120 g

B12 Work out

(a) 5% of £60 (b) 5% of £200 (c) 5% of 140 g (d) 5% of 240 ml

B13 Work out

(a) 15% of 20 kg (b) 35% of 300 g (c) 65% of 60 eggs (d) 45% of 160 g

B14 5% of the weight of a seeded grape is pips.
If you buy 500 g of seeded grapes, what weight is pips?

B15 15% of the weight of cherries is stones.
If you buy 400 g of cherries, what weight is stones?

B16 95% of the weight of raw tomatoes is water.
How much water is there in 300 g of raw tomatoes?

B17 When Luigi bought some pasta he got '15% extra free'.

(a) A normal pack weighs 500 g. How much extra did he get?

(b) What was the **total** weight of the pack he bought?

B18 These labels show the percentage of fat in some foods.

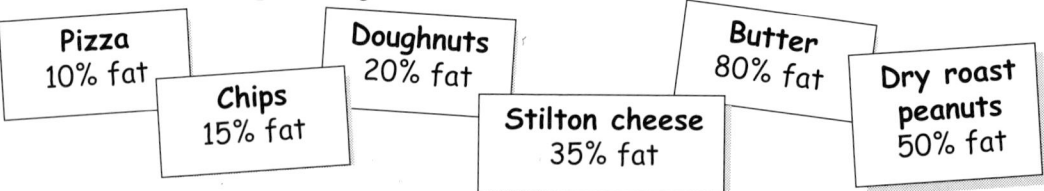

How much fat is there in

(a) a 250 g pizza   (b) a 30 g doughnut   (c) 120 g of dry roast peanuts
(d) 200 g of butter   (e) 400 g of chips   (f) 250 g of dry roast peanuts
(g) 500 g of Stilton cheese (h) 60 g of chips   (i) 300 g of Stilton cheese

B19 A cake is described as '85% fat free'

(a) What percentage of the cake is fat?

(b) If the cake weighs 400 g, how much fat does it contain?

C Percentages on a calculator

To calculate 36% of £450.

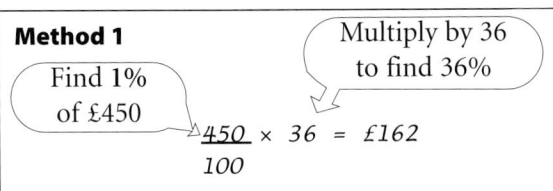

Method 1
Find 1% of £450 — Multiply by 36 to find 36%
$$\frac{450}{100} \times 36 = £162$$
On a calculator: 450 ÷ 100 × 36 = 162

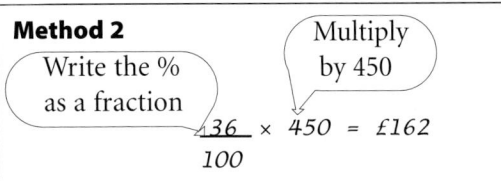

Method 2
Write the % as a fraction — Multiply by 450
$$\frac{36}{100} \times 450 = £162$$
On a calculator: 36 ÷ 100 × 450 = 162

Method 3
$36\% = \frac{36}{100} = 0.36$ so on a calculator $0.36 \times 450 = 162$

C1 Calculate
(a) 36% of 200 (b) 74% of 250 (c) 44% of 350 (d) 72% of 550

C2 Calculate
(a) 22% of 80 (b) 64% of 120 (c) 48% of 70 (d) 86% of 340
(e) 17% of 240 (f) 39% of 880 (g) 23% of 420 (h) 92% of 820

C3 Find
(a) 23% of £85 (b) 47% of £56 (c) 33% of £84 (d) 83% of £54

C4 Find
(a) 36% of 94 litres (b) 84% 0f 450 g (c) 17% of 350 ml (d) 93% of 150 km

C5 14% of a fried egg is fat.
How much fat is there in a fried egg weighing 45 g?

C6 8% of brown bread is protein.
How much protein is there in an 800 g loaf of brown bread?

C7 This is some nutritional information about some different food.

Food	Water	Fat	Protein	Carbohydrate
Cheddar cheese	36%	34%	26%	0%
Tofu	51%	18%	24%	2%
Corn flakes	3%	1%	8%	86%

How much is there of
(a) water in 250 g of Cheddar cheese
(b) protein in 225 g of tofu
(c) carbohydrate in 35 g of corn flakes
(d) fat in 120 g of Cheddar cheese
(e) fat in 280 g of tofu
(f) water in 750 g of cornflakes

D One number as a percentage of another

> 7 out of a class of 25 students cycle to school.
> What percentage is this?
> Write as a fraction and make the denominator 100
>
> $\frac{7}{25}$ cycle
>
> $\frac{7}{25} = \frac{28}{100} = 28\%$ (× 4)

> Out of 200 tyres checked 90 were found to be faulty. What percentage is this?
>
> $\frac{90}{200}$ are faulty
>
> $\frac{90}{200} = \frac{45}{100} = 45\%$ (÷ 2)

D1 Write these as percentages
(a) 7 out of 20 (b) 12 out of 25 (c) 13 out of 50 (d) 13 out of 20

D2 Write these as percentages
(a) 150 out of 200 (b) 75 out of 500 (c) 650 out of 1000 (d) 160 out of 400

D3 Ray takes 20 bottles to the bottle bank.
4 of the bottles are brown. What percentage are brown?

D4 A pack contains 10 pens of which 5 are black, 3 are blue and 2 are red.
What percentage of the pens are
(a) black (b) blue (c) red (d) not red

D5 A 25 g cereal bar has these listed under 'nutrition':

Protein 3 g   Carbohydrate 16 g   Fat 4 g   Fibre 2 g

What percentage of the bar is
(a) protein (b) carbohydrate (c) fat (d) fibre

D6 Tina scored 30 out of 50 in her Maths exam.
Mel scored 65% in the same Maths exam.
Who got the better score? Explain your answer.

D7 In a survey on holidays 160 out of 200 people said they preferred to go abroad.
What percentage prefer to go abroad?

D8 A school has 600 students and 90 were absent.
What percentage were absent?

D9 (a) Write 60 out of 80 as a fraction.
(b) What is this fraction in its simplest form?
(c) What is 60 out of 80 as a percentage?

D10 For each of these
- write it as a fraction
- change the fraction to its simplest form
- write the fraction as a percentage

(a) 30 out of 60 (b) 10 out of 40 (c) 33 out of 60 (d) 36 out of 80

E Calculating percentages

Jason had £125 birthday money and spent £45 of it on a computer game.
What percentage of his money did he spend?

Write it as a fraction
$$\frac{45}{125}$$

Divide to change to a decimal
$$45 \div 125 = 0.36$$

Multiply by 100 to change to a %
$$0.36 \times 100 = 36\%$$

On a calculator
$$45 \div 125 \times 100 = 36$$
So 45 out of 125 is 36%

E1 Work these out as percentages
  (a) 56 out of 160   (b) 63 out of 225   (c) 54 out of 72   (d) 364 out of 560
  (e) 36 out of 40   (f) 75 out of 250   (g) 3 out of 75   (h) 228 out of 240

E2 A triathlon had 120 entries but only 78 actually finished the race.
  (a) What percentage finished the race?   (b) What percentage dropped out?

E3 Ms King marks her Art exam out of 80. Change these marks out of 80 to percentages:
  Miriam 68   Charles 36   Adam 56   Tak Man 72   Celia 44

E4 A survey of 150 students on their choice of school uniform colour gave these votes
  Black 81   Blue 27   Grey 30   Green 12
  What **percentage** voted for each option?

E5 Azmat's garden is a rectangle measuring 15 m by 10 m.
  In the garden he digs a rectangular vegetable patch 3 m by 7 m.
  (a) What is the area of (i) his whole garden
                           (ii) his vegetable patch
  (b) What percentage of his garden is taken up by his vegetable patch?

Worked example

A 27 g crunchy bar contains 7 g of fat.
Find the percentage of the bar which is fat to the nearest 1%.

$$7 \div 27 \times 100 = 25.92592592 \quad \text{which is 26\% to the nearest 1\%}$$

E6 Write these as percentages to the nearest 1%.
  (a) 27 out of 48   (b) 43 out of 80   (c) 35 out of 78   (c) 23 out of 75
  (e) 45 out of 56   (f) 28 out of 65   (g) 210 out of 560 (h) 25 out of 48

E7 Paul lists how many hours each day he spends on different activities.
  Sleeping 8   School 7   Eating 2   Homework 3   Television 4
  Work these out as percentages of the whole day.
  Check that they add to 100%.

F Mixed questions

F1 A 330 ml carton of drink contains 5% blackcurrant juice and 4% apple juice.
How many ml in the carton is
(a) blackcurrant juice
(b) apple juice

F2 Fried fish fingers contain

55% water   15% protein   15% fat   15% carbohydrate

(a) How much fat is there in 250 g of fried fish fingers?
(b) How much water is there in 250 g of fried fish fingers?

F3 Dermot's garden is a rectangle measuring 15 metres by 5 metres
(a) What is the total area of the garden?
(b) The lawn takes up 55% of the garden. What is the area of the lawn?
(c) A flower bed is a rectangle measuring 3 m by 2 m.
What percentage of the garden is this?

F4 A rectangular carpet measures 2.40 m by 1.75 m.
62% of the area of the carpet is red.

Calculate the area of the red carpet.
Give your answer to a suitable degree of accuracy.

AQA 2003 Specimen

F5 In a survey a group of people were asked how they learned how to use a computer.
The answers were listed as

Reason	Number of people
Self taught	33
Through work	18
From family or friend	5
At school	21
Other	3

(a) How many people were asked in the survey in total?
(b) What percentage of this total were self taught?
(c) What percentage learned at school?

*F6 These are the results of a survey on students who had passed their driving test.

	Passed first time	Took more than one test
Male	7	17
Female	9	16

(a) What is the total number of females in the survey?
What percentage of these passed first time?
(b) What is the total number of males in the survey?
What percentage of these passed first time?
(c) How many people, males and females, took part in the survey altogether?
What percentage of these were female?

Test yourself with these questions

T1 (a) Write $\frac{3}{4}$ as a percentage.

(b) Write 30% as a fraction.

Edexcel

T2 (a) A frozen curry weighs 380 g.
The curry contains 25% meat.
What weight of meat does it contain?

(b) An individual frozen pie weighs 160 g.
The pie contains 28% meat.
What weight of meat does it contain?

OCR

T3 In an election there were three candidates.
The candidates were Alan Archer, Priti Patel and Simon Smith.

Alan Archer got 25% of the votes, Priti Patel got 35% of the votes and Simon Smith got the rest.

(a) What percentage of the votes did Simon Smith get?

(b) Who won the election?

Altogether 40 000 people voted in the election.

(c) How many people voted for Priti Patel?

OCR

T4 Jo did a maths test.
There was a total of 40 marks for the test.
Jo got 65% of the marks.

(a) Work out 65% of 40.

Jo got 36 out of 80 in an English test.

(b) Work out 36 out of 80 as a percentage.

Edexcel

T5 In a hockey tournament, the Gladiators team was awarded 40 corners.
It scored from 30 of them

(a) What percentage is this?

(b) The Allstars team scored from 35 out of 50 corners.

Which is the better team at scoring from corners?
Give a reason for your answer.

OCR(MEG)

T6 A cake is made from fat, flour and sugar.
The cake weighs 110 g.
The weight of the sugar is 42 g.
What percentage of the cake is sugar?
Give your answer correct to one decimal place.

AQA(SEG) 1998

14 Coordinates

You will revise
- how to use coordinates in all four quadrants

You will learn
- how to complete shapes on coordinate grids
- how to find the midpoint between two sets of coordinates
- how to describe points in space using 3D coordinates

A Shapes on grids

The diagram shows three points A, B and C.
- What are the coordinates of A, B and C?
- Where could you put two new points R and S so that line RS is parallel to BC?
- Where could you put two new points P and Q so that line PQ is parallel to AB?
- If ABC are three corners of a rectangle, what are the coordinates of the 4th point D?
- What could the coordinates of the 4th point D be if ABCD was a trapezium?

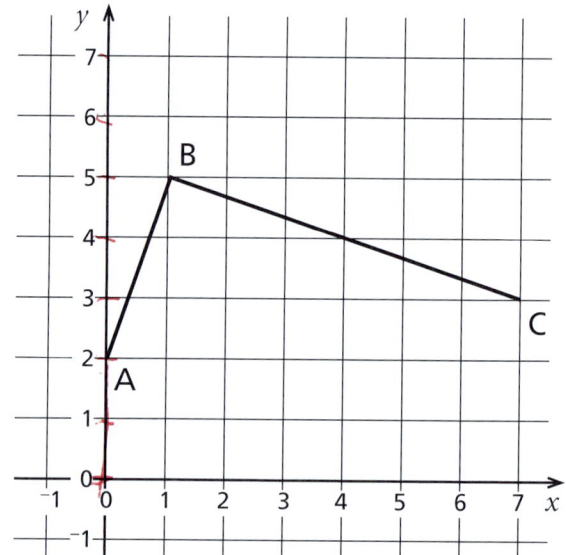

A1 The diagram shows three points, E, F and G.
Copy this diagram with x- and y-axes going from -5 to 7.

(a) M is point (4, 3).
Mark a point N on your graph so that MN is parallel to FG.

(b) Give the coordinates of two points K and L so that KL is parallel to EF.

A2 (a) Mark a new point H so that EFGH is a square.

(b) The line with equation $x = 3$ is a line of symmetry for the square. What other line is a line of symmetry?

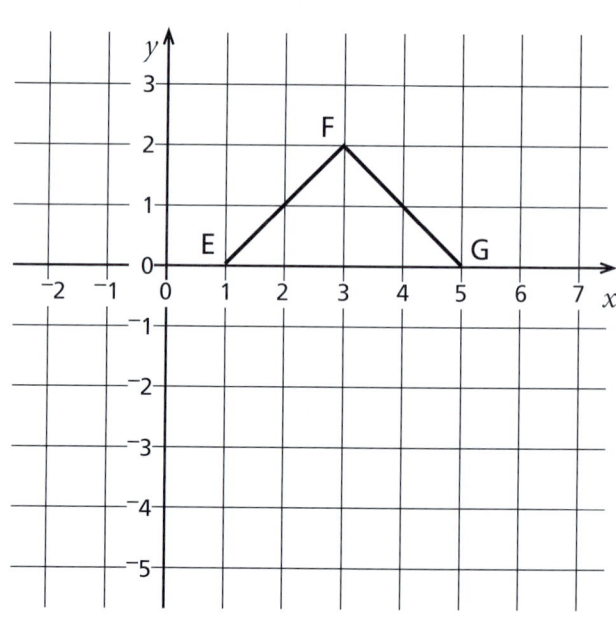

120 • 14 Coordinates

A3 The diagram shows three points, I, J and K.
Copy this diagram with x and y axes
going from ⁻5 to 7.

(a) Mark a point L so that IJKL is a parallelogram.

(b) What would be the coordinates of point L if
IJKL was a kite?

(c) What line of symmetry would this kite have?

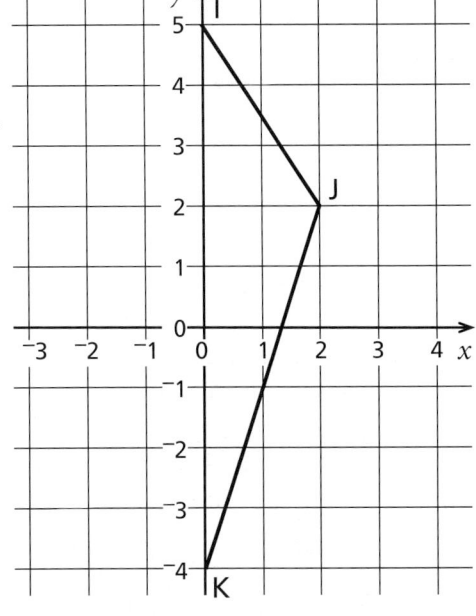

A4 (a) Draw a grid on squared paper with the x- and y-axes going from ⁻4 to 7.
Mark points A (1, 3), B (3, 6) and C (5, 3)

(b) What would the coordinates of point D be if ABCD is a rhombus?

(c) What could the coordinates for D be if ABCD is a kite?

(d) What is the equation of the line of symmetry of the kite in (c)?

A5 (a) On your grid mark points E(3, ⁻2), F(1, ⁻4) and G(⁻3, ⁻2)

(b) What would the coordinates of point H be if EFGH is a parallelogram?

(c) What would the coordinates of point H be if EFGH is a kite?

(d) Describe the line of symmetry of the kite in (c).

A6 MNOPQ is a pentagon.
The y-axis is a line of symmetry of the pentagon.
Three of the points are M(0, 3), N(3, 1), O(2, ⁻2).

(a) Draw a grid with x- and y-axes going from ⁻5 to 7.
Plot points M, N and O.

(b) Use this to find the coordinates of P and Q.

B Mid-points

Stuck in the middle

A game for two players

Sheet P136 has a game board with a grid and 'targets'.

- The first player says the coordinates of a point on the grid.
  The second player then places a cross at that point.
  You cannot change your mind once you have said a point.

- The second player then says a point for the first player to mark with a cross.
  If one of the targets is exactly halfway between the new cross and any other marked cross the second player wins the target.
  Write your initial in any target you win.

- Players then take it in turns to give new points until all the targets have been won.
  You can win more than one point in any one go.

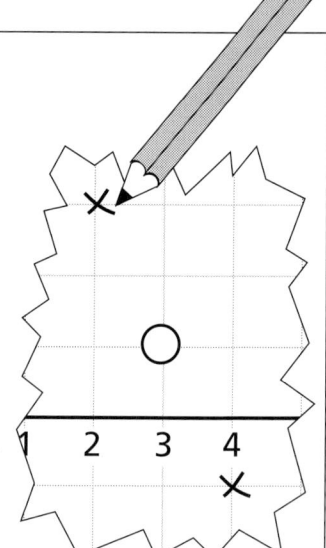

B1 Write down three different pairs of coordinates that would win the point (6, 5).

B2 Write down three different pairs of coordinates that would win the point (2, −3).

B3 Write down what number is halfway between the pairs below.
You may find this number line useful.

```
  −5  −4  −3  −2  −1   0   1   2   3   4   5
```

(a) 2 and 4   (b) 6 and 10   (c) 12 and 20   (d) 1 and 3
(e) 1 and 5   (f) 13 and 19   (g) 2 and 5   (h) 11 and 18
(i) −4 and −2   (j) −1 and −6   (k) −9 and −6   (l) −5 and 3
(m) −2 and 4   (n) −3 and 4   (o) −5 and 2   (p) −8 and 12

To find the midpoint between two coordinates, for example A(−2, 3) and B (4, −5)

- Find the midpoint of the *x* coordinates: midpoint of −2 and 4 is 1
- Find the midpoint of the *y* coordinates: midpoint of 3 and −5 is −1

So the point exactly half way between A and B is (1, −1).
Check using a grid that this is true.

B4 There are four points on a grid

A (3, 2)   B (5, 8)   C (3, 0)   D (1, 5)

Without drawing, work out the coordinates of the points that are halfway between

(a) A and B   (b) B and C   (c) A and C   (d) A and D.

B5 There are four points on a grid

P (6, 4)   Q (3, −2)   R (−3, −4)   S (−1, 5)

Write down the coordinates of the points that are halfway between

(a) P and Q   (b) Q and R   (c) S and R   (d) S and P

B6 (a) Draw a grid with x- and y-axes going from −7 to 7.

(b) Draw the kite whose corners are at (1, 3), (4, 6), (7, 3) and (4, −3)

(c) Mark the midpoint of each side of this quadrilateral.

(d) Join the mid-points up to make a new quadrilateral.
What type of quadrilateral is the new one?

B7 On the same grid as B6

(a) Draw the quadrilateral whose corners are at (−1, 1), (−7, 1), (−4, 5) and (−2, 5)

(b) What type of quadrilateral is this?

(c) Mark the midpoint of each side of this quadrilateral.

(d) Join the mid-points up to make a new quadrilateral.
What type of quadrilateral is the new one?

Side splitting

What are the midpoints of the sides of this quadrilateral?

Copy this shape onto squared paper.

Join the midpoints to make a new quadrilateral.

Draw some quadrilaterals of your own on grids. Join up the midpoints of the sides of each quadrilateral to make a new shape.

What do you find?

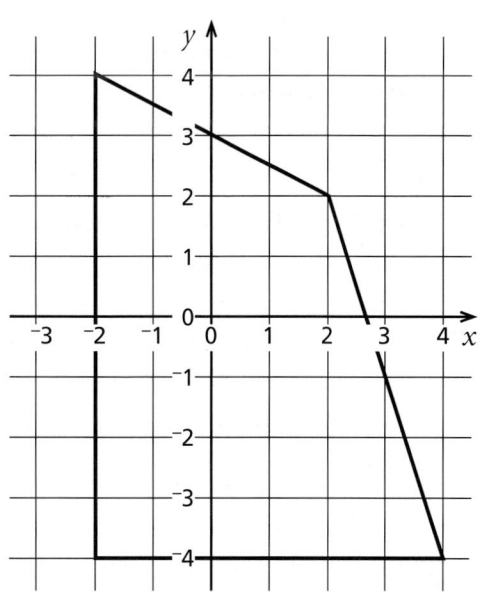

C 3-D coordinates

To give the position of a point in 3-D space a third axis is needed, called the z-axis.
So each point has three coordinates, written in the form (x, y, z).

Making your own grid

- Cut out the 3-D grid from sheet P137 and stick it together.
  Place it with the x-axis and the y-axis on the desk and the z-axis pointing upwards.

- Here a rod 3 units high has been placed on the grid.
  The bottom of the rod has coordinates $(2, 4, 0)$.
  What are the three coordinates of the
  top of the rod?

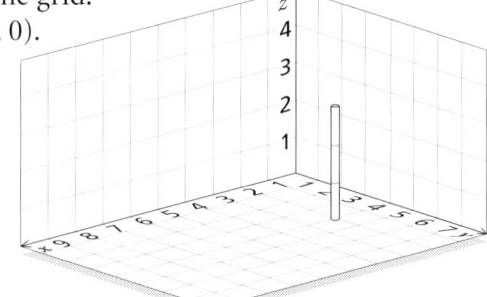

- Cut out the rectangle from sheet P138.
  Place it on the bottom of the 3-D grid with its x-axis and y-axis matching the grid.
  What are the coordinates of P, Q, R and S? (Give three coordinates for each point.)

- Lift the rectangle up 3 units. What are the coordinates of P, Q, R and S now?

- Cut out the net for the cuboid from sheet P138 and
  glue it together.
  Place the cuboid on the 3-D grid like this
  (corner B is at $(0, 0, 0)$ and face P is
  at the bottom).
  What are the coordinates of each corner
  that you can see?

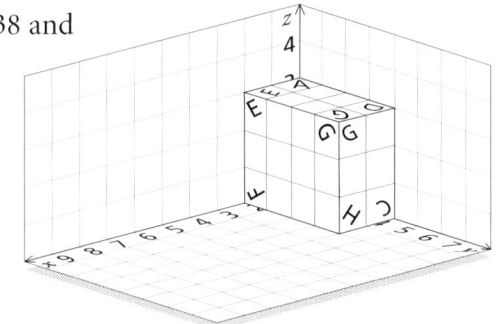

C1 Place the cuboid on the 3-D grid with corner A at $(0, 0, 0)$ and face M at the bottom.
Write down the coordinates of the corners
(a) F   (b) C   (c) E   (d) H

C2 Place the cuboid with corner C at $(0, 0, 0)$ and face N at the bottom.
Write down the coordinates of the corners
(a) B   (b) G   (c) E   (d) A

C3 Place the cuboid so that point A is at $(5, 2, 0)$,
point D is at $(1, 2, 0)$ and face M is at the bottom.
Write down the coordinates of the corners
(a) G   (b) B   (c) F   (d) H

C4 On this 3-D grid there are some centimetre cubes.

Write down the 3D coordinates of points A, B, C, D and E.

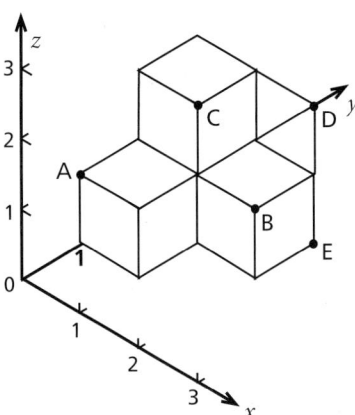

In the room

Choose a point in your classroom that could be (0, 0, 0).
Use a metre rule to mark axes along the edges of the room with chalk or tape.

Write down the 3-D coordinates of points in your classroom.

Test yourself with these questions

T1 (a) Draw a grid with the x and y axes going from $^-6$ to 6.
Plot the points A($^-3$, 2), B($^-1$, 4) and C(3, 1)

(b) What would be the coordinates of point D if ABCD is a parallelogram?

(c) Plot the point E(5, $^-4$).
What type of quadrilateral is ABCE?

T2 ABC is a triangle where A is point ($^-2$, $^-1$), B is (4, 3) and C is (6, $^-2$).
Give the coordinates of the midpoints of sides

(a) AB (c) BC (c) CA

T3 The diagram shows 8 one-centimetre cubes fixed together.

Corner A has coordinates (1, 1, 0).

Write down the coordinates of points B and C.

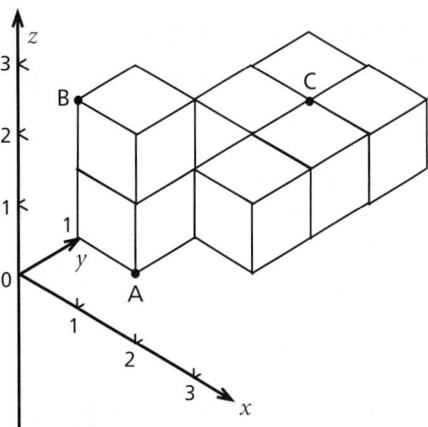

OCR(MEG)

15 Using a calculator 1

You will revise

◆ how to decide whether to add, subtract multiply or divide.

You will learn

◆ how to use a calculator to help solve a problem

A Which calculation?

- Which of these calculations goes with each problem below?

  (Some calculations may be used twice and some not at all!)

  312 + 39   39 – 312   312 – 39

  312 × 39   39 ÷ 312   312 ÷ 39

A Josh sold plants at a school fair.
When the fair started he had 312 plants to sell.
He had 39 left at the end of the fair.
How many plants did Josh sell?

B There are 39 rooms in a school.
Each room is to have a smoke alarm.
Alarms cost £312 each.
How much will the alarms cost altogether?

C A school hires coaches to take children on a trip.
Each coach takes 39 children.
312 children are going on the trip.
How many coaches are needed?

D Sheila has 39 people working for her.
She buys them each a bottle of wine for Christmas.
The wine costs £312 altogether.
How much does each bottle cost?

E Dilip delivers leaflets to houses.
He went out on Saturday with a bag of leaflets.
He delivered 312 leaflets.
Afterwards he had 39 leaflets left in his bag.
How many leaflets did he have in his bag when he started?

F A school is selling tickets for a show.
So far 39 tickets have been sold.
There are 312 tickets that have not yet been sold.
How many tickets are there altogether?

A1 Each room in an office block has 48 light bulbs.
If there are 27 rooms, how many light bulbs are there altogether?

A2 The distance by rail from London to Edinburgh is 405 miles.
A train on its way from London to Edinburgh is 188 miles from London.
How far is the train from Edinburgh?

A3 Paul's truck can hold 28 tonnes of coal.
He has to move 420 tonnes of coal from one place to another.
How many journeys does he need to make?

A4 Errol buys a carpet whose area is 14.6 square metres.
The carpet costs £13.45 per square metre.
How much does Errol pay?

A5 A group of 48 people hire a coach and agree to share the cost equally.
The coach hire costs £600. How much does each person pay?

A6 Ronnie bought some 27p stamps.
He paid £6.75 altogether.
How many stamps did he buy?

A7 Karen is arranging a picnic lunch for 8 people.
She spends £12.45 on sandwiches, £1.89 on crisps and £3.26 on drinks.

(a) What is the total cost of the picnic?

(b) The 8 people agree to share the total cost equally.
How much does each person pay?

A8 Hayley buys 6 ices and 4 lollies.
She pays £6.70 altogether.
The ices cost 75p each.

(a) How much did the 6 ices cost altogether?

(b) What was the cost of the 4 lollies?

(c) How much did each lolly cost?

A9 Here is the menu at Lou's cafe.

Burger	£1.29
Cheeseburger	£1.59
Doughnut	69p

Jack bought 3 burgers, 2 cheeseburgers and some doughnuts.
He paid £9.81 altogether.

(a) How much did the burgers and cheeseburgers cost altogether?

(b) How much did the doughnuts cost altogether?

(c) How many doughnuts did Jack buy?

A10 Here are the ticket prices for Fab Funfair.

Mr Blake and his two children are going to the Funfair.
So are Mr Patel and his two children.

Adult £16.55
Child £12.85
Group ticket
(2 adults and up to 4 children)
£70

(a) How much will the Blakes and the Patels pay altogether if they go in separately?

(b) How much will each family save if the two families go in together as a group?

B Showing working

Worked example

Paul sends his daughter to post 6 identical parcels.
He gives her a £20 note and she comes back with £4.52 change.
How much did each parcel cost to post?

Cost of posting 6 parcels = £20 − £4.52 = £15.48
Cost of posting each parcel = £15.48 ÷ 6 = **£2.58**

B1 SCARY PARK
Adult £19
Child £13

Here are the ticket prices for entry to Scary Park.
A group of 7 adults and 15 children visit the park.
How much do they pay altogether?

B2 Sandra buys a desk, a chair and a lamp.
The desk costs £57.95. The chair costs £24.75.
The total cost of all three things is £101.25.

How much does the lamp cost?

B3 When Sarah goes on a business trip she claims 34p for every mile she drives.

She drives on business from her home to Birmingham (73 miles), then from Birmingham to Manchester (89 miles) and finally back home (112 miles).

(a) How far did she travel altogether?

(b) How much can she claim for this journey?

B4 Here is part of the menu at a Chinese restaurant.

8 people have a meal.

They order 3 crispy seaweed, 3 sesame prawn toast,
2 sweet and sour pork, 3 beef chow mein,
2 Peking duck and 5 fried rice.

Crispy seaweed	£3.25
Sesame prawn toast	£3.95
Sweet and sour pork	£4.50
Beef chow mein	£4.95
Peking duck	£8.85
Fried rice	£1.85

They share the total cost of the meal equally.
How much does each person pay?

B5 Kylie bought 12 tins of blue paint and 9 rolls of wallpaper.
She remembered that each tin of paint cost £4.89 and the total bill came to £93.60.

How much did each roll of wallpaper cost?

B6 Gail is going to make fruit cakes to sell at a fair.
She spends the following amounts on the ingredients:

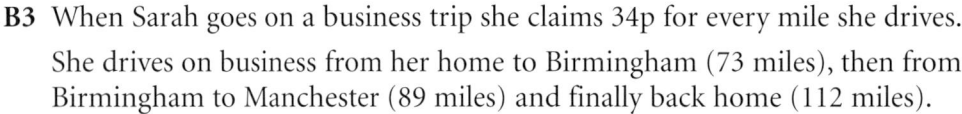

Flour **£5.40**   Sugar **£3.75**   Butter **£4.90**   Eggs **£11.80**   Dried fruit **£13.20**

Gail makes 24 cakes from these ingredients.
She sells them at £3.75 each. All the cakes are sold.

(a) How much profit does Gail make?

(b) How much does the dried fruit for one cake cost?

B7 Rachel bought a ringbinder, paper and some felt-tips.
The ringbinder cost £3.49, the paper £2.75 and the felt-tips were 37p each.

The total cost was £11.42.

How many felt-tips did Rachel buy?

B8 A family of 2 adults and 3 children is going to London by train.
The normal fares are:

　　　　Adult **£14.80**　　　Child **£8.20**

If the family buys a 'Family Railcard', they get reduced fares:

　　　　Adult **£9.90**　　　Child **£2.00**

The family decide to buy the 'Family Railcard'.
It costs £20, but they get the reduced fares.

If they only use the Railcard this one time, how much do they save by buying it and getting the reduced fares?

C *Changing money*

If you go abroad, you may need to change your money into a different currency.

Suppose the exchange rate between the pound and the US dollar is **£1 = US$1.35**

To change pounds to dollars you **multiply by 1.35**

　　　　　　£60 ⟶ × **1.35** ⟶ $81

> The number of dollars must be greater than the number of pounds.

To change dollars to pounds you **divide by 1.35**

> The number of pounds must be less than the number of dollars.

　　　£60 ⟵ ÷ **1.35** ⟵ $81

C1 Bharat goes to Canada. The exchange rate is £1 = 2.32 Canadian dollars.

(a) He changes £120 into Canadian dollars. How many dollars does he get?

(b) When he leaves Canada, he changes 73.50 dollars into pounds.
The exchange rate is the same.
How much does he get, to the nearest penny?

C2 The exchange rate between the pound and the Swiss franc is £1 = 2.38 Swiss francs.

Change　(a) £33.60 to Swiss francs　(b) 88.70 Swiss francs to £, to the nearest penny

C3 The exchange rate between the pound and the Japanese yen is £1 = 178 yen.

Change　(a) £64 to yen　　　　(b) 850 yen to £, to the nearest penny

C4 The exchange rate between the pound and the Australian dollar is £1 = 2.95 dollars.

Change　(a) £240 to dollars　　(b) 850 dollars to £, to the nearest penny

D Comparing costs

Worked example

A 2 kg bag of new potatoes costs £1.34.
A 2.5 kg bag costs £1.59.

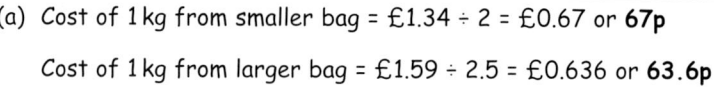

(a) What is the cost of 1 kg in each bag?

(b) Which bag gives you more potatoes for your money? Explain why.

(a) Cost of 1 kg from smaller bag = £1.34 ÷ 2 = £0.67 or **67p**

Cost of 1 kg from larger bag = £1.59 ÷ 2.5 = £0.636 or **63.6p**

(b) The larger bag gives you more for your money, because 1 kg costs less.

D1 Steve paid £6.40 for a box of 10 computer disks.
Sheila paid £7.80 for a box of 12 of the same type of disk.

Who got the better bargain? Explain your answer.

D2 A 3.5 kg bag of barbecue charcoal costs £5.25.
A 5.5 kg bag costs £8.49.

Which size gives you more for your money? Explain your answer.

D3 Maiden Cola is sold in three sizes.

A 1.5 litre bottle costs £1.32,
A 2.5 litre bottle costs £2.25.
A 3 litre bottle costs £2.79.

(a) Calculate the cost of 1 litre in the largest bottle.

(b) Calculate the cost of 1 litre in the middle bottle.

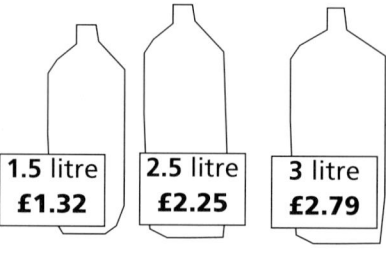

(c) Calculate the cost of 1 litre in the smallest bottle.

(d) Which bottle is best value?

D4 Runners Crisps are sold in two sizes.

A normal pack costs 25p and contains 60 grams.
A big pack costs 40p and contains 100 grams.

(a) How many grams do you get for 1p in the normal pack?

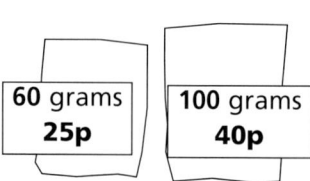

(b) How many grams do you get for 1p in the big pack?

(c) Which pack is better value? Explain why.

D5 Carrots are sold in bags and sacks.
Bags of carrots weigh 3 kg and cost 72 pence.
Sacks of carrots weigh 14 kg and cost £2.66.

How much, per kilogram, is saved by buying sacks of carrots instead of buying bags of carrots?

AQA(SEG) 1999

D6 There are three ways of buying cans of Buxter's lemonade:

| Individual cans cost 35p each. | A 6-pack (six cans) costs £1.75. | You can buy five 6-packs for the price of four |

(a) If you buy one 6-pack, how much does each can cost, to the nearest penny?

(b) If you buy five 6-packs what does each can cost, to the nearest penny?

(c) How much do you save altogether by buying five 6-packs rather than the same number of individual cans?

Test yourself with these questions

T1 Venus chocolate bars cost 28p each.
A special Christmas tin contains 16 bars and costs £4.99.

If you buy the tin instead of 16 separate bars, how much are you paying for the tin itself?

T2

QAQ GAS SUPPLIES CHARGES

Standing charge 7p per day

Gas used 41p per unit

Rachel's gas meter was read on 1 March.
The reading was 1 7 4 2

92 days later the meter was read again.
The reading was 1 9 5 6

Calculate the total gas bill that Rachel will have to pay for the 92 days from 1 March.

AQA 2003 Specimen

T3 A computer magazine is published every month and costs £2.99 per copy.
If you place a regular order you can get the magazine for three months for a cost of £5.49.
Chris buys the magazine for a year by paying for three months at a time.
During the year, how much would be saved using this method rather than buying a copy every month?

WJEC

T4 Mel changes £150 into New Zealand dollars. The exchange rate is £1 = 3.30 NZ dollars.

(a) How many New Zealand dollars does she get?

When she leaves New Zealand, Mel changes 76 NZ dollars to pounds.
The exchange rate is now £1 = 3.18 NZ dollars.

(b) How much does Mel get, to the nearest penny?

T5 The weights and prices of two tins of pineapple are shown.

Which tin of pineapple gives more grams per penny?

You **must** show all your working.

227 g
27 pence

432 g.
52 pence

AQA(SEG) 2000

16 Brackets

You will revise
- how to simplify expressions like 2a + 3 – a + 5, 2n + 3m – n + 2m or 4s × 2t

The work will help you learn
- how to multiply out brackets
- how to factorise expressions using brackets

A Review

A1 Work out these expressions when $a = 2$, $b = 3$ and $c = 4$.
(a) ab (b) $5c$ (c) $2(b + c)$ (d) $2b + c$ (e) $2(c - b)$
(f) $\frac{1}{2}(a + c)$ (g) $a + 2b$ (h) $ab - 4$ (i) $10 - 2b$ (j) $3c - 2b$

A2 Simplify each of these expressions
(a) $u + u + u$ (b) $v + 4 + v$ (c) $1 + w + 5 + w + 2$
(d) $u + 5 + u - 3$ (e) $v + 3 + v - 1 + v$ (f) $w + 12 + w - 5 + w$

A3 Simplify
(a) $4a + 7a$ (b) $14 + 3b + 5b$ (c) $6c + 5 - 2c + 3$
(d) $4d + 2 - d + 5 + 3d$ (e) $2e + 5 + 5e - 2 - 3e$ (f) $7 + 5f - 4 - 2f$

A4 Simplify
(a) $4a + b + 2a + 7b$ (b) $10 + 2b + 5b + 3c$ (c) $5c + 6d + 4 - 2c + 2d$
(d) $4d + 2 + 4e - 3 + 3d$ (e) $2e + 7f + 9e - 4f + 3e$ (f) $6g + 2f + 4h + 5f - g + h$

A5 Find and simplify an expression for the perimeter of each of these shapes.

(a)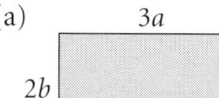
(b)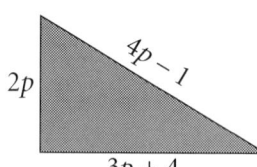
(c)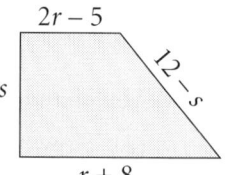

A6 Write each expression as simply as possible
(a) $5x - 2x + 9x - x$ (b) $3y - 9 + 2y + 5 + 4y$
  OCR

A7 Simplify $4x + 3x + 7y - 2x + 3y$
  AQA 2000

A8 Simplify (a) $n \times n$ (b) $2a \times a$ (c) $2s \times 3s$ (d) $k \times 5k$ (e) $4u \times 5u$

A9 Simplify (a) $2x \times y$ (b) $a \times 3b$ (c) $2s \times 3t$ (d) $u \times v$ (e) $4u \times 5v$

B Expressions with brackets

Here is a box of crisps.
We don't know how many packets are in one box.
So let n stand for the number of packets in a box.

Here is one box and 2 more packets
So here we have $n + 2$ packets.

Here are 3 lots of: a box and 2 packets.   It is the same as 3 boxes and 6 packets.

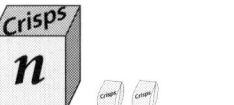

$3(n + 2)$ and $3n + 6$ are called **equivalent expressions**.

B1 There are three pairs of equivalent expressions here.
Pair them up and find the odd one left over.

$2(x + 4)$ $2(x + 16)$ $2x + 4$ $2(x + 8)$ $2x + 16$ $2(x + 2)$ $2x + 8$

B2 There are three pairs of equivalent expressions here.
Pair them up and find the odd one left over.

$3a + 18$ $3(a - 2)$ $3a - 6$ $3(a + 6)$ $3a - 18$ $3(a - 6)$ $3a - 2$

B3 Multiply out the brackets in each of these expressions
(a) $2(x + 5)$ (b) $3(y + 3)$ (c) $5(p - 6)$ (d) $10(7 + q)$ (e) $4(v - 5)$

Each term inside the brackets
is multiplied by the number outside. $5(3x + 4) = 5 \times 3x + 5 \times 4 = 15x + 20$.

B4 Multiply out the brackets in each of these expressions.
(a) $3(2x + 4)$ (b) $2(4y - 3)$ (c) $6(1 + 3p)$ (d) $6(1 - 3p)$ (e) $8(5 - 3v)$

B5 Find what is missing in each of these.
(a) $2(a + 6) = 2a + \blacktriangle$ (b) $\blacksquare(b + 2) = 3b + 6$ (c) $4(c + \bullet) = 4c + 20$

16 Brackets • 133

C Factorising

The reverse of multiplying out an expression is called **factorising** an expression.

Notice that you should make the factor outside the brackets as big as you can.

Factorise $6a + 18$
$6a + 18$
$= 6(a + 3)$

Factorise $12a - 16$
$12a - 16$
$= 4(3a - 4)$

C1 What is the largest whole number that divides exactly into
(a) 12 and 16   (b) 20 and 18   (c) 12 and 24   (d) 14 and 21

C2 Copy each of these, filling in the missing numbers.
(a) $6a + 8 = \blacksquare(3a + 4)$ (b) $10b - 15 = \blacklozenge(2b - 3)$ (c) $14c + 6 = \blacktriangledown(7c + 3)$

C3 Factorise each of these expressions.
(a) $2x + 8$ (b) $3y + 9$ (c) $5p - 15$ (d) $20 + 4q$ (e) $12v - 24$

C4 Factorise each of these as far as you can.
(a) $6x + 9$ (b) $8x + 12$ (c) $25 - 15x$ (d) $9x + 12$ (e) $8x - 28$

C5

E	G	H	O	N	A	T	R	S
2	3	4	5	$x + 3$	$2x + 3$	$x + 15$	$3x + 2$	$3x + 6$

Factorise each of these expressions into two factors.
Use the code above to find the letter for each factor.

$4x + 6$ $5x + 15$ $9x + 6$

For example, $4x + 6 = 2(2x + 3)$.
The two factors are 2 and $2x + 3$. So your first two letters are E and A.

Rearrange your letters to make the name of a fruit.

C6

S	C	D	E	P	N	W	R	U	O
2	3	4	5	6	7	$x + 1$	$2x + 1$	$2x + 3$	$3x + 4$

Factorise the expressions in each part as far as you can.
Use the letters in the table above to find three flowers.

(a) $6x + 8$ $10x + 5$
(b) $4x + 6$ $6x + 3$ $9x + 12$
(c) $7x + 7$ $4x + 2$ $18x + 24$ $12x + 16$

D More letters

Sometimes a **letter** may be the factor outside a bracket.

Worked examples

Multiply out $w(w + 3)$
$w(w + 3)$
$= w \times w + w \times 3$
$= w^2 + 3w$

Expand $a(2a - 3)$
$a(2a - 3)$
$= a \times 2a - a \times 3$
$= 2a^2 - 3a$

Factorise $n^2 + 4n$
$n^2 + 4n$
$= n \times n + n \times 4$
$= n(n + 4)$

Factorise $3m^2 - 5m$
$3m^2 - 5m$
$= m \times 3m - m \times 5$
$= m(3m - 5)$

D1 Copy each of these, filling in what is missing.
(a) $a(a + 4) = a^2 + \blacksquare$
(b) $b(2b - 3) = 2b^2 - \blacktriangledown$
(c) $c(1 + c) = c + \blacklozenge$

D2 Multiply out each of these expressions.
(a) $n(n + 3)$
(b) $m(m - 4)$
(c) $r(1 + 2r)$
(d) $s(4s - 3)$
(e) $x(3x + 4)$
(f) $y(3 - 5y)$

D3 Multiply out
(a) $4v(v + 5)$
(b) $2w(w - 4)$
(c) $2x(x + 1)$
(d) $3y(2 - y)$

D4 There are two pairs of equivalent expressions here, and one left over.
Find the three pairs, and multiply out the one left over.

| $n(2n + 3)$ | $n^2 + n$ | $n(3n + 2)$ | $2n^2 + 3n$ | $n(n + 1)$ | $3n^2 + 2n$ | $n(2n + 1)$ |

D5 Copy each of these, filling in what is missing.
(a) $n(\blacktriangledown + 2) = n^2 + 2n$
(b) $\blacksquare(n + 3) = n^2 + 3n$
(c) $n(n + \blacklozenge) = n^2 + 4n$

D6 Factorise each of these expressions as fully as you can.
(a) $m^2 + 9m$
(b) $n^2 - 5n$
(c) $2x^2 + x$
(d) $3y^2 - 5y$
(e) $3p + 4p^2$
(f) $2q - 5q^2$
(g) $2v^2 + 4v$
(h) $18w^2 - 4w$

Sometimes when you multiply out a bracket there may be more than one letter inside.

Just multiply each term inside by whatever is outside.

Expand $3(a + 2b)$
$3(a + 2b)$
$= 3 \times a + 3 \times 2b$
$= 3a + 6b$

Expand $4(2x - 3y)$
$4(2x - 3y)$
$= 4 \times 2x - 4 \times 3y$
$= 8x - 12y$

D7 Expand these expressions.
(a) $2(a + b)$
(b) $3(f - e)$
(c) $4(2g + h)$
(d) $3(k - 3g)$
(e) $4(2h + 3j)$
(f) $5(2w + u)$

D8 Factorise these expressions.
(a) $3a + 3b$
(b) $3g - 6h$
(c) $7k + 14l$
(d) $5w + 15z$

E Simplifying

To simplify an expression containing brackets, first multiply out the brackets.

Worked examples

Simplify $4 + 2(a + 3)$	Simplify $2a + 3(a - 4)$	Simplify $4(2a + 3) + 5a$	Simplify $2(a - 3) + 5(2a + 1)$
$4 + 2(a + 3)$	$2a + 3(a - 4)$	$4(2a + 3) + 5a$	$2(a - 3) + 5(2a + 1)$
$= 4 + 2a + 6$	$= 2a + 3a - 12$	$= 8a + 12 + 5a$	$= 2a - 6 + 10a + 5$
$= 2a + 10$	$= 5a - 12$	$= 13a + 12$	$= 12a - 1$

E1 Simplify the following expressions.
 (a) $3(z + 5) + 4$ (b) $5 + 10(b + 2)$ (c) $2(x + 8) + 3x$
 (d) $2y + 3(4 + y)$ (e) $6(a - 3) + 2a$ (f) $2(4 - c) + 4c$

E2 Simplify the following expressions.
 (a) $3x + 2(2x + 4)$ (b) $4(3w + 2) + 3w$ (c) $15 + 2(5 + 3z)$
 (d) $4u + 2(2u - 3)$ (e) $4(3 - 5v) - 10$ (f) $50 + 12(3w - 4)$

E3 There are three pairs of equivalent expressions here. Can you find them?

P $2x + 3(2x + 3)$ **Q** $4(2x + 3) - 6$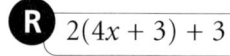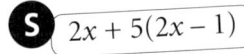

T $3(4x - 1) - 2$ **U** $4x + 2(2x + 3)$

E4 Simplify.
 (a) $2(a + 3) + 3(a + 2)$ (b) $4(b - 1) + 2(b + 3)$ (c) $2(5 + c) + 4(2c - 2)$

E5 This puzzle is on sheet P139.

F Subtracting

When subtracting an expression with brackets, you need to be careful about the signs.

Worked examples

Simplify $8 - (a + 3)$	Simplify $8 - (a - 3)$	Simplify $5a - 2(a + 4)$	Simplify $5a - 2(a - 4)$
$8 - (a + 3)$	$8 - (a - 3)$	$5a - 2(a + 4)$	$5a - 2(a - 4)$
$= 8 - a - 6$	$= 8 - a + 3$	$= 5a - 2a - 8$	$= 5a - 2a + 8$
$= 2 - a$	$= 11 - a$	$= 3a - 8$	$= 3a + 8$

F1 Simplify each of these expressions.
 (a) $15 - (a + 2)$ (b) $8b - (2b + 5)$ (c) $12 - (c - 4)$
 (d) $6d - (3d - 2)$ (e) $12 - (1 + 3e)$ (f) $6f - (8 - 2f)$

F2 Simplify each of these.
(a) $12 - 2(n + 3)$
(b) $7n - 3(n - 2)$
(c) $10 - 5(n - 2)$
(d) $8n - 3(2 + n)$
(e) $8n - 3(2 - n)$
(f) $15 - 3(5 - n)$

F3 Simplify these expressions.
(a) $2x + 5 - (x + 2)$
(b) $4(h + 2) - (3h - 1)$
(c) $3(j - 1) - 2(1 + j)$
(d) $5(x + 3) - 3(x + 2)$
(e) $3(y + 4) - 2(y - 5)$
(f) $6(z + 4) - 4(z + 5)$

F4 There are three pairs of equivalent expressions here, and an odd one out. Which is the odd one out?

$(4x + 3) - (2x + 1)$
$3(x + 3) - 2(x + 1)$
$3(2x + 1) - (4x + 1)$
$2(3x + 1) - 5(x - 1)$
$(2x - 3) - (x + 1)$
$3(x + 2) - 2(x + 1)$
$3(x - 2) - 2(x - 1)$

G Mixed examples

G1 Expand each of these expressions.
(a) $3(s + 4)$
(b) $2(a - 3)$
(c) $4(2 + t)$
(d) $5(2u - 4)$
(e) $4(2e + 3)$

G2 Factorise as much as you can
(a) $3r + 6$
(b) $5s - 25$
(c) $6a + 8$
(d) $4 - 6u$
(e) $18t + 12$

G3 Factorise as fully as possible
(a) $s^2 + 4s$
(b) $3d^2 + 6d$
(c) $4h^2 - 8h$
(d) $4h^2 - h$
(e) $6j^2 + 9j$

G4 Simplify
(a) $4a \div 2$
(b) $6b^2 \div 3$
(c) $\dfrac{8c}{2}$
(d) $\dfrac{12a}{2}$
(e) $\dfrac{12a^2}{6}$

G5 Expand and simplify
(a) $2(f + 4) + 3f$
(b) $12 + 3(a - 2)$
(c) $10 + 5(1 - b)$
(d) $4(g - 3) + 6g$
(e) $12 - (t + 2)$
(f) $12u - (4 + u)$
(g) $15 - 3(s + 1)$
(h) $4a + 15 - 2(a - 2)$

G6 Expand and simplify
(a) $s + 3(s + t)$
(b) $3a + 4b + 2(a + b)$
(c) $2n - 3m + 3(n + m)$

G7 Simplify
(a) $a + a + a + a$
(b) $4p + 2p$
(c) $7t + 3s - 5t + s$ Edexcel

Expand and simplify
(d) $3(2m + 2)$

G8 (a) Simplify $a + 3a + 5a$
(b) Solve $7b = 56$ AQA 2003 Specimen

G9 (a) This rectangle has area $2(a + 3b)$.
Multiply out $2(a + 3b)$.

(b) This rectangle has area $3a + 12$.
The width of the rectangle is 3.

Write down an expression for the length of the rectangle.

OCR

G10 (a) Simplify $4p + 2p$
(b) Simplify $7t + 3s - 5t + s$
(c) Expand and simplify $3(2m + 2) - 2(m - 3)$

Edexcel

G11 (a) Expand $5(x - 4)$ (b) Expand $x(3 - x)$

Edexcel

*****G12** This puzzle is on sheet P140.

Test yourself with these questions

T1 Expand (a) $3(d + 4)$ (b) $5(u - 2)$ (c) $4(2 + s)$ (d) $2(3 - y)$

T2 Multiply out (a) $2(3e + 2)$ (b) $6(3p - 2)$ (c) $3(1 + 2w)$ (d) $3(1 - 2w)$

T3 Factorise (a) $3x + 6$ (b) $7a - 14$ (c) $6 + 12b$ (d) $5 - 10t$

T4 Simplify
(a) $12 + 2(a + 1)$ (b) $8a + 2(3 - a)$ (c) $10 - (2 + t)$ (d) $6x - (2x - 3)$
(e) $3a + 2(3a - 3)$ (f) $12 + 3(4a + 2)$ (g) $8v - 2(3v + 4)$ (h) $15 - 3(1 - 2h)$

T5 Expand
(a) $d(d + 2)$ (b) $u(u - 4)$ (c) $h(2h + 3)$ (d) $j(3j - 7)$
(e) $3(s + 2t)$ (f) $4(d - 3w)$ (g) $3(2e - 2f)$ (h) $5(3k + 2g)$

T6 Factorise (a) $x^2 + 6x$ (b) $a^2 - 14a$ (c) $6a + 12b$ (d) $5s - 10t$

T7 (a) Simplify (i) $x + 3x + x$ (ii) $6x \div 2$ (iii) $y \times 3y$
(b) Multiply out (ii) $4(x + y)$ (ii) $5(x - 2y)$

AQA(SEG) 1998

T8 (a) Expand $5(x - 4)$
(b) Write down an expression for the total length of the line.
Give your answer in its simplest form.

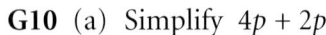

Edexcel

17 Pie charts

You should know
- how to work with fractions and percentages
- how to measure angles
- that the angles at the centre of a circle add up to 360°

You will learn how to
- draw and interpret pie charts

A Review

A1 In a class of 24 students there are 12 who have been to Spain on holiday.
(a) What fraction of the students have been to Spain?
(b) What percentage of the students is this?

A2 In a group of 40 college students only 10 of them eat breakfast.
(a) What fraction of these students eat breakfast?
(b) Write this fraction as a percentage.

A3 In a primary school 60 children are met by a grandparent at the end of the day. The school has 360 pupils.
What fraction of the pupils are met by a grandparent?

A4 (a) What fraction of this circle is shaded grey?
(b) Calculate the size of the angle in the sector shaded black.
(c) What percentage of the circle is white?

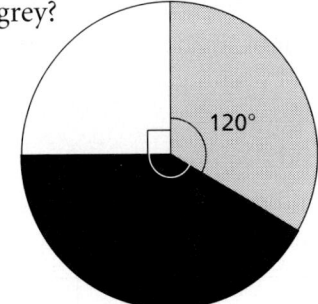

A5 Calculate (a) $\frac{1}{3}$ of 360   (b) $\frac{1}{4}$ of 360   (c) $\frac{1}{5}$ of 200   (d) $\frac{1}{8}$ of 160

A6 In a secondary school, $\frac{1}{4}$ of the students like swimming. 200 students like swimming.
How many students in total go to this school?

A7 Calculate (a) 25% of 180   (b) 20% of 300   (c) 40% of 300

A8 Calculate (a) 13% of 400   (b) 56% of 250   (c) 28% of 1400

B Reading pie charts, simple fractions and percentages

B1 This chart shows sales of ice-creams at a school fete.
The total number of ice-creams sold was 600.

(a) What flavour sold the least ice-creams?

(b) What fraction of the ice-creams sold were chocolate?

(c) How many ice-creams sold were chocolate?

(d) What fraction of the ice-creams were vanilla?

(e) How many vanilla ice-creams were sold?

(f) Calculate the size of the angle for the strawberry ice-creams.

(g) How many strawberry ice-creams were sold?

(h) How many mint ice-creams were sold?

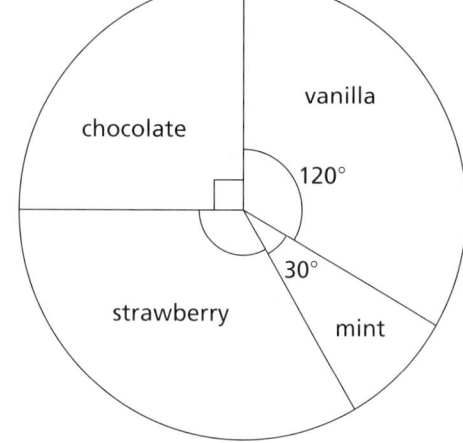

B2 This pie chart shows how Heather spent a typical Monday.

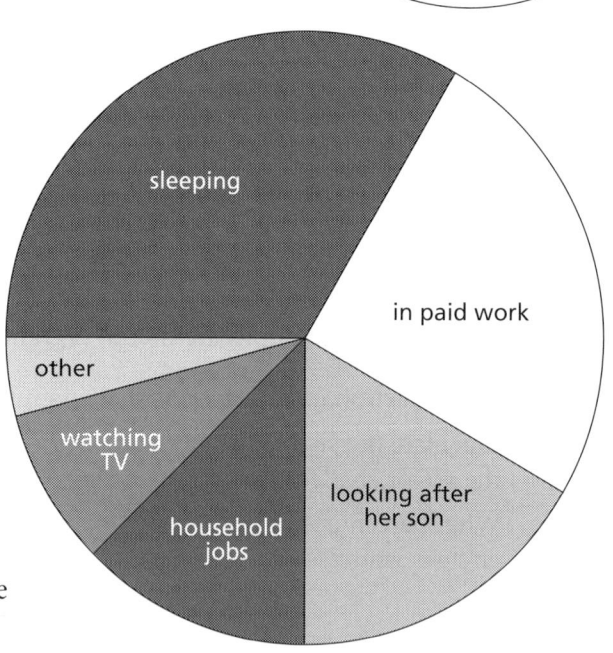

(a) Measure the angle for the time she spent sleeping.

(b) What fraction of the day did she spend sleeping?

(c) How many hours did she spend sleeping?

(d) (i) Copy and complete this table for Heather's day.

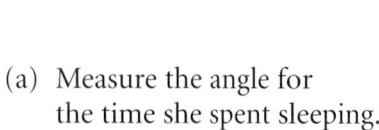

Activity	Angle	Number of hours
Sleeping		
In paid work		

(ii) Check that the total number of hours is 24.

B3 In a survey, Year 11 pupils were asked the question:

'Where do you learn the most?'

Their replies are shown in the pie chart below.

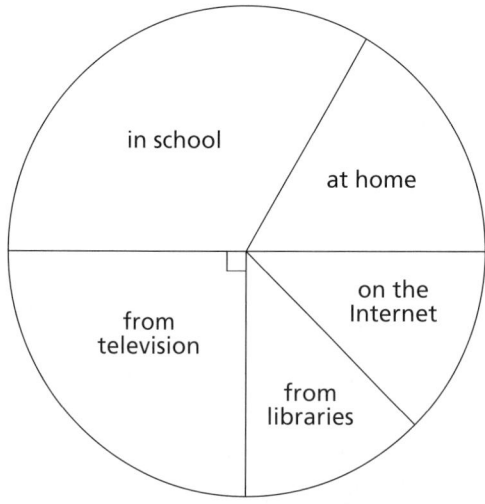

(a) What was the most common reply to the question?

(b) What percentage of pupils said they learnt most from television?

(c) What fraction of the pupils said they learnt most at home?

AQA 1999

B4 The pie chart shows how the cost of a holiday was shared between various items.

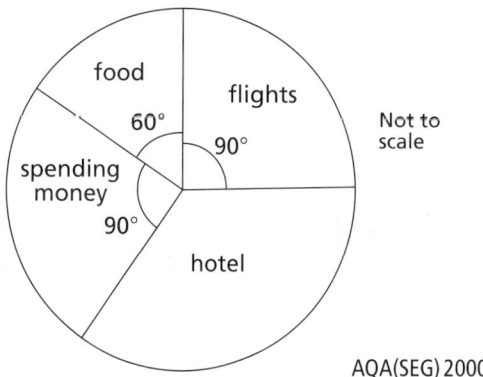

The flights cost £600.

(a) Calculate the total cost of the holiday.

(b) (i) **Calculate** the size of the angle which represents the cost of the hotel.

(ii) Calculate the cost of the hotel.

AQA(SEG) 2000

B5 The pie chart gives information about the sales of music CDs at a store one Saturday.

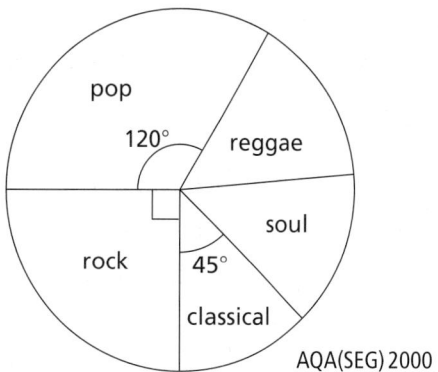

(a) What fraction of the CDs sold were Pop CDs?

(b) 40 Classical CDs were sold.

(i) How many CDs were sold altogether?

(ii) How many Rock CDs were sold?

AQA(SEG) 2000

17 Pie charts • 141

C Reading pie charts: the unitary method

900 school students were asked:
  'What is the first thing you usually do when you get home from school?'
Their replies are shown in the pie chart below.

How many students usually have a snack?

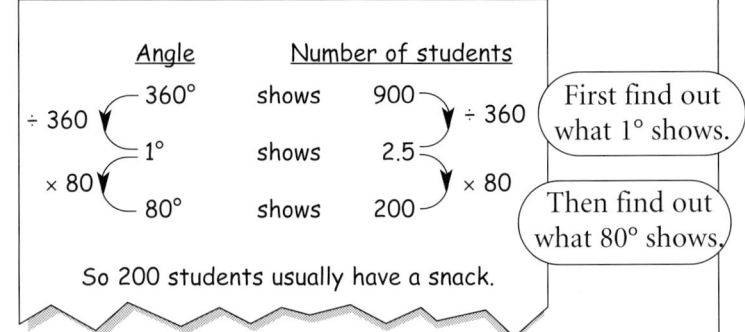

So 200 students usually have a snack.

C1 720 cars were sold at an auction.
The pie chart shows the countries where they were made.

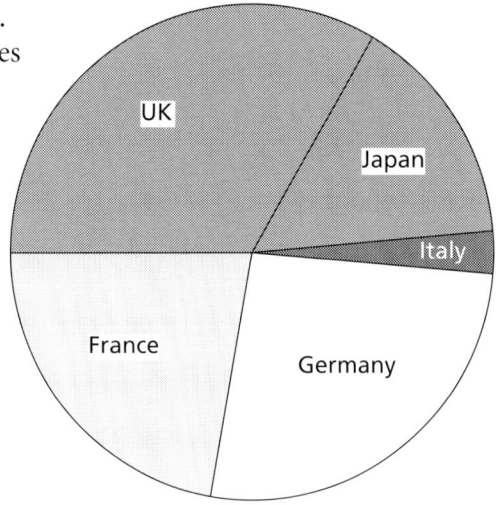

(a) In which country were most of these cars made?
(b) How many cars are represented by 1°?
(c) (i) Measure the angle for the cars made in France.
    (ii) How many of the cars sold were made in France.
(d) Work out the number of cars made in
    (i) Germany   (ii) Japan   (iii) UK   (iv) Italy

C2 In a school, 288 students were asked:

'What colour would you like for the school sweatshirt?'

The pie chart shows the results.

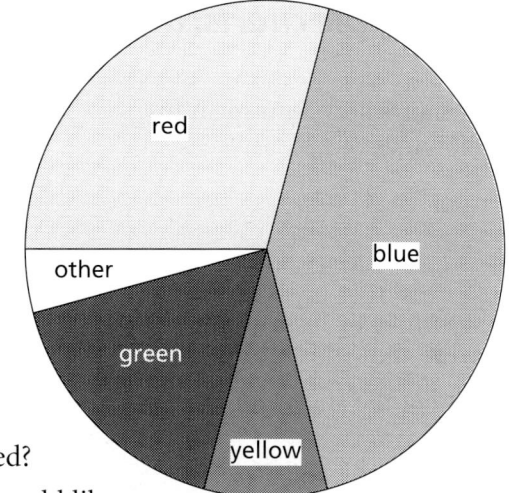

(a) What colour was the mode?

(b) (i) Measure the angle for red.

   (ii) How many people would like red?

(c) Work out the number people who would like

   (i) blue   (ii) green   (iii) yellow

C3 Sue records the ducks she sees on a pond one afternoon. The pie chart shows her results.

(a) What fraction of these ducks were Mallards?

She sees 36 Mallards.

(b) How many ducks did Sue see altogether?

(c) How many Teals did she see? Show your working clearly.

(d) (i) Calculate the angle for Shovelers.

   (ii) How many Shovelers did she see?

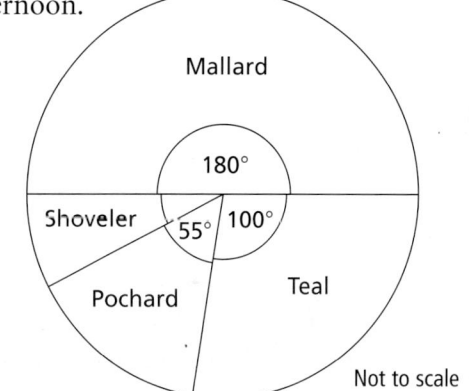

C4 The pie chart shows the different types of trees in a wood.

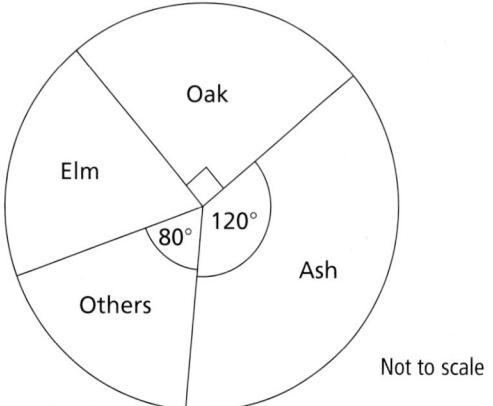

(a) What fraction of the trees in the wood are Ash?

There are 459 Oak trees in the wood.

(b) How many trees are in the wood altogether?

(c) How many Elm trees are there?

AQA(SEG) 1999

D Drawing pie charts: angles

This table shows how Tom spent his weekly allowance of £20 last week.

Item	Amount
Clothes	£8
Savings	£5
Music	£4
Magazines and sweets	£3

We can use an angle measurer to draw a pie chart to show this information.

First, work out the angles to use.

÷ 20 ⤵ £20 is shown by 360°
        £1 is shown by 18° ⤴ ÷ 20

Divide 360° by 20 to work out the angle for £1.

Item	Amount	Angle
Clothes	£8	8 × 18° = 144°
Savings	£5	5 × 18° = 90°
Music	£4	4 × 18° = 72°
Magazines and sweets	£3	3 × 18° = 54°
Totals	£20	360°

Work out the total as a check.

D1 Kenny records the eye colour of the people in his class.

(a) How many people are in his class?

(b) In a pie chart, what angle will represent 1 person?

(c) What will be the angle for people with blue eyes?

(d) Work out all the angles and draw the pie chart. Label each sector.

Colour	Frequency
Brown	10
Blue	4
Green	3
Grey	1

D2 Sam is a car salesman. He records the number of cars of each make that he sells in a month.

Draw and label a pie chart to represent this information.

Make	Frequency
Ford	16
Rover	10
Vauxhall	6
BMW	4

AQA 2000

D3 In an English lesson, the 24 pupils in a class were each asked to write down the first vowel in their name.

The table shows the information.

First vowel in a pupil's name	Number of pupils
A	6
E	3
I	5
O	8
U	2

The information can be shown in a pie chart.
Construct the pie chart. *Edexcel*

D4 Karen did a survey to find the most popular cereal.

The table shows the three most popular cereals and other cereals eaten by adults.

Cereal	Muesli	Weeta Bites	Cornflakes	Other cereals
Number of adults	20	15	30	25

Draw a clearly labelled pie chart to illustrate this information. *AQA(SEG) 2000*

D5 This question is on sheet P141.

D6 Pali asked 180 boys what was their favourite sport.
Here are his results

Sport	Soccer	Rugby	Cricket	Basketball	Other
Number of adults	74	25	18	37	26

(a) Draw a pie chart to show these results.

Pali also asked 90 girls about their favourite sport.
In a pie chart showing the results, the angle for Tennis was 84°

(b) How many of these girls said that Tennis was their favourite sport? *OCR*

E Drawing pie charts: percentages

This table shows how Tom spent his weekly allowance of £20 last week.

Item	Amount
Clothes	£8
Savings	£5
Music	£4
Magazines and sweets	£3

We can use a pie chart scale to draw a pie chart to show this information.

First, work out the percentages to use.

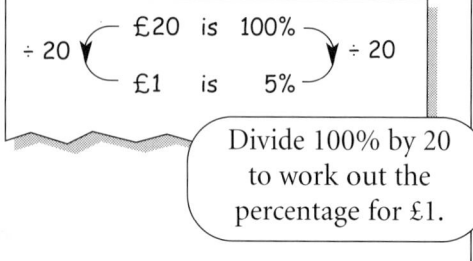

Divide 100% by 20 to work out the percentage for £1.

Item	Amount	Percentage
Clothes	£8	8 × 5% = 40%
Savings	£5	5 × 5% = 25%
Music	£4	4 × 5% = 20%
Magazines and sweets	£3	3 × 5% = 15%
Totals	£20	100%

Work out the total as a check.

E1 This table shows the percentage of plain chocolate which is water, protein, fat or carbohydrate.

Water	Protein	Fat	Carbohydrate
1%	5%	29%	65%

Draw and label a pie chart to show this information.

OCR

E2 Keith records the eye colour of the people in his class.

(a) How many people are in his class?

(b) What percentage of the class is 1 person?

(c) What percentage of the class has blue eyes?

(d) Work out all the percentages and draw the pie chart. Label each sector.

Colour	Frequency
Brown	13
Blue	8
Green	3
Grey	1

E3 Paul asked 50 boys what was their favourite fruit.

Here are his results.

Fruit	Apple	Orange	Banana	Grapes	Other
Number of boys	8	6	20	9	7

(a) Draw a pie chart to show these results.

Paul also asked some girls about their favourite fruit.
This pie chart shows the results.

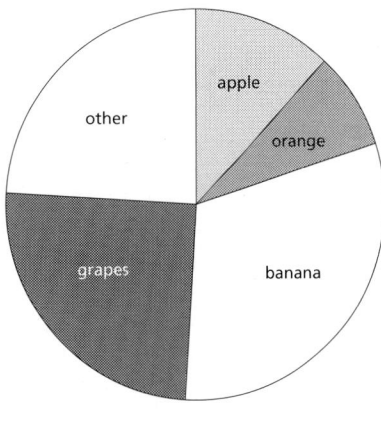

(b) State one way in which the girls' and boys' results are similar.

(c) State one way in which the girls' results are different from the boys' results.

OCR

E4 This table shows the percentage of people of different categories injured in road accidents in one English county.

Category	Percentage of people injured in road accidents
Car occupants	62
Pedestrians	11
Cyclists	12
Motorcyclists	10
Occupants of heavy vehicles	5

(a) Altogether 8859 people were injured. How many car occupants were injured?

(b) This table shows the **number** of people of different categories injured in one town.

Category	Number
Vehicle occupants	72
Pedestrians	45
Cyclists	18
Motorcyclists	15

Draw and label a pie chart to represent this information. Show your working.

OCR

F Handling real data

Beth and Geeta are working on a project on eating habits.

Beth investigates pre-prepared meals …

I eat pre-prepared meals …	Number of people
… always	8
… usually	10
… sometimes	23
… never	5

- Can you show this information in a pie chart?

… and Geeta looks at vegetarian meals.

I eat vegetarian meals …	Number of people
… always	5
… usually	11
… sometimes	43
… never	2

- Can you show this information in a pie chart?

- Try one of these surveys in your class.
  Compare the results for your class with Beth or Geeta's.

F1 Julia asked 150 people what was their favourite crisp flavour.

Flavour	Ready salted	Salt and vinegar	Cheese and onion	Other
Number of people	21	50	64	15

(a) Draw a pie chart to show this information.

(b) Try Julia's survey on your class and draw a pie chart to show the information.
How do the results of your survey compare with Julia's?

F2 Ken asked his classmates what was their favourite fruit.

Fruit	Apple	Banana	Orange	Grape	Other
Number of people	5	10	3	6	3

(a) How many people are in Ken's class?
(b) Draw a pie chart to illustrate this information.

F3 In a 1996 survey, a total of 2975 families with dependent children were asked who looked after the children.

Here are the results.

Main carers	Number of families
Couple	2352
Widowed, divorced or separated mother	357
Single mother	208
Lone father	58

Draw a pie chart to show these results.

F4 In a 1996 survey, a total of 9128 people were asked what type of home they lived in.

Here are the results.

Type of home	Frequency
Detached house	1917
Semi-detached house	2921
Terraced house	2465
Flat or maisonette	1825

Draw a pie chart to show these results.

Test yourself with these questions

T1 The pie chart shows the reasons given by 24 pupils for being late for school.

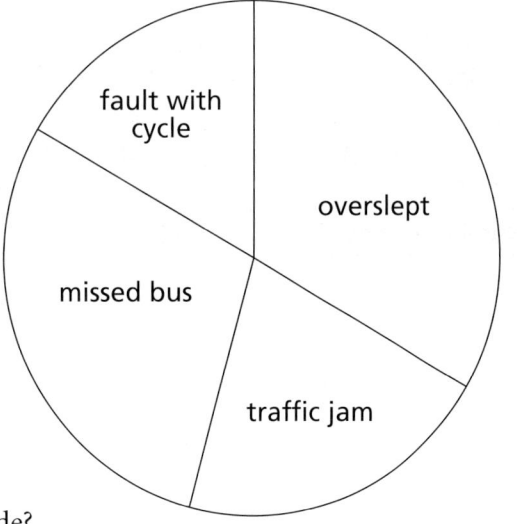

(a) Which reason for lateness is the mode?
(b) Use the pie chart to work out how many of these pupils said they overslept.

AQA(SEG) 1998 Specimen

T2 Sophie conducts a survey in her class to find out about computer use.

Here are her results.

Have own	9
Share	6
Use only in school	10
Never use	5
	30

Show this information in a pie chart.
Label each sector. AQA 2000

T3 One Saturday a newsagent sells the following:

National daily newspapers	510
Echo	360
Magazines and comics	210

Draw a clearly labelled pie chart to represent these sales. AQA(SEG) 1998

T4 Yvonne recorded the makes of 50 cars that were parked in Edgedale Road.

These are her results.

Make of car	Number
Ford	12
Vauxhall	18
Rover	6
Toyota	5
Other	9

Draw and label a pie chart to illustrate this information. OCR

Review 2

1. This recipe makes 5 pancakes.
   (a) How much flour would you need to make one pancake?
   (b) Write out a list of what you would need to make 10 pancakes.
   (c) Harry has a kilogram of flour, a litre of milk, 6 eggs and lots of salt. How many pancakes can he make?

   Plain pancakes
   100 grams plain flour
   250 ml milk
   1 egg
   $\frac{1}{2}$ teaspoon salt
   Method: sift the flour and salt into a bowl, make a well in the centre and add the egg. Stir in half the

2. Jeff has 120 cows.
   He has two children, John (aged 4) and Harriet (aged 8).
   In Jeff's will, he leaves his cows to his two children.
   The cows are to be divided in the ratio of the children's ages.
   (a) If Jeff dies today, how many cows will each child get?
   (b) If Jeff dies in 4 years time, how many cows will they each get?

3. Choose the most appropriate unit from the ones below for giving
   (a) the weight of a railway engine.
   (b) the weight of a piece of paper
   (c) the weight of a sheep
   (d) the height of the Eiffel tower
   (e) the distance from London to Paris
   (f) the width of a pencil

   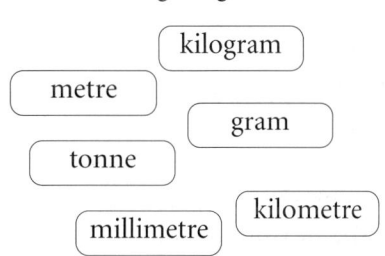

4. Copy and complete
   (a) 5 miles = … kilometres
   (b) 1 inch is about 2.5 …
   (c) 2.2 … is about 1 kilogram
   (d) 1 gallon is about … litres

5. The diagram shows the results of a survey of the number of people in cars passing a school.
   (a) What is the modal number of people in each car?
   (b) How many cars passed the school during the survey?
   (c) How many people were in these cars altogether?

   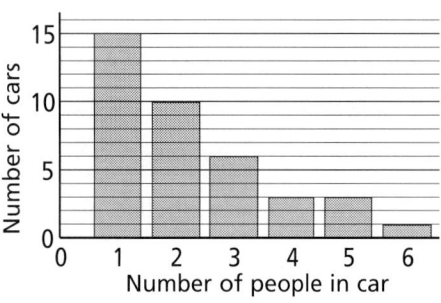

6 This table shows the numbers of boys and girls present in a class one day.

	Present	Absent	Totals
Boys	8	2	
Girls	15		
Totals			30

  (a) How many boys should there be in the class when they are all there?
  (b) How many girls are in the class altogether?
  (c) Copy and complete the table.
  (d) What fraction of the girls were absent that day?
  (e) What percentage of the boys were absent?

7 Work out
  (a) $3 + {}^-2$ (b) ${}^-3 - {}^-2$ (c) ${}^-3 \times 2$ (d) ${}^-3 \times {}^-2$
  (e) $4 \times {}^-3$ (f) $20 \div {}^-2$ (g) ${}^-20 \div {}^-2$ (h) $({}^-10)^2$

8 Calculate
  (a) 24% of £150   (b) 16% of 35 g   (c) 48% of 550 m   (d) 98% of 15 km

9 In her end-of-term tests, Harriet got 45 out of 80 for Maths; 37 out of 70 for English and 46 out of 85 for History.

Which subject did she do best in? Explain.

10 Draw a grid with both x and y going from ${}^-3$ to 3.
On your grid, plot the points A $({}^-1, 2)$, B $(2, 3)$, C $(3, {}^-2)$ and D $({}^-3, {}^-2)$.
  (a) Mark the midpoints of each side of ABCD. Join these mid-points to form a new quadrilateral.
  (b) What type of quadrilateral is the new one?

11 *Value* baked beans come in three sizes.
  (a) Which size tin gives you more for your money? Explain your answer.
  (b) Rachel buys six of the 454 gram tins. How much change does she get from £5?

150 g
18 p

200 g
20 p

454 g
44 p

12 Multiply out and simplify   (a) $3(x + 2) + 5$ (b) $5(2m - 1) + 3$ (c) $a(a + 2)$

13 Factorise fully   (a) $3a + 12$ (b) $4b + 6$ (c) $c^2 + 5c$

14 This table shows how a group of people get to work.

Method	Car	Bike	Bus	Train	Walk
Number of people	9	5	2	3	1

Draw a clearly labelled pie-chart to show this information.